I'M FROM ARTHUR AVENUE!

My Bronx Boyhood and Beyond

FRANK LUCIDO

COPYRIGHT DOCUMENTS

Copyright © 2024: Frank Lucido
All Rights Reserved.
ISBN: 979-8-3306-0193-6

No part of this publication may be reproduced, distributed, or transmitted in any form or by any means, including photocopying, recording, or other electronic or mechanical methods, without the prior written permission of the publisher, except in the case of brief quotations embodied in critical reviews and certain other noncommercial uses permitted by copyright law.

Case Number: 1-13319700618

TABLE OF CONTENTS

Prologue: My stories, fact or fiction?	1
Author's Note	4
EARLY YEARS	
A Four-year-old's Perspective	6
Charlie Beans	10
Southern Boulevard	15
Eddie the Carpenter	20
LIFE BEYOND The Bronx	
Country Living	26
Hugh Hicks and "Mr. Charlie"	30
ON THE MOVE	
Our World Falls Apart	34
A Dark Time for Us	38
The Donisis	39
MY FATHER'S UNIVERSE	
The Shack	43
In the Driver's Seat	46
The Ugliest Day In My Life	50
Payment in Full	52
An Unsanctioned Hit	55
SCHOOL DAZE	
Public School and Me	59
After-school Activities	62
TURNING POINTS	
Angela	68
Joel Schreibman	71
Irwin Goldberg	73
Moving On	76

FRANKIE BEANS

Counterfeiting	79
Prison Time	82
Not Yet on the Straight and Narrow	87
"Mafia! Mafia! Mafia!" (I Start a Rent Strike)	91

LIVING A NORMAL LIFE

Settling Down	95
"My Mind Says Yes, but My Heart Says No"	97
Establishing a Business	99
Scenes From Eddie's Album	105
Tangling With Mr. Harold Little Phil Sorts It Out	109
Starting Over	114

PETER PICCIANO

Piermont	117
Carlo's Death	121
The Pole Vault	122

SICILIAN ROUTES

Heritage	127
Lercara Friddi	130

THE LUCK OF THE DRAW

Eddie's Children	137
One Chromosome	141
Epilogue: You Can Take the Boy Out of The Bronx, but You Can't Take The Bronx Out of the Boy	145
Acknowledgments	148

For my sons, Paul and David, and my grandchildren, Charlotte and Dylan. And for all those who may come after.

Prologue

MY STORIES, FACT OR FICTION?

In his eighty-third year, now old and frail, my father finished his Christmas dinner with my family. My two sons, Paul and David, hadn't seen much of their grandfather while growing up. What they knew of him, they learned from the many stories I told them over the years. Most of the time, they viewed these as fiction from a son, bragging about his father. On Christmas day, at my home in suburban New York, their opinion changed.

Paul had invited two of his college friends to share the evening with us. After dinner, my younger son, David, set up his music stand to play some Christmas songs for us on his clarinet. While waiting for David, the adults were reminiscing about Grandpa Charlie and his various talents. From the corner of my eye, I caught Paul in his playful way, goofing on our conversation, as if it was time for my tall tales, once again.

After several of David's musical selections, my wife noticed that my Dad was crying. She turned to him,

"Charlie, what's the matter? Are you okay?"

"I'm fine. I can't believe how good he is," he replied.

"Why shouldn't he be good? He has your musical talent!" She continued warmly, addressing the rest of the family and guests. "You know that Grandpa Charlie could have been many things, and one of them was an opera singer!"

My father, now composed, didn't disagree. "One night, after I sang at the annual Ferragosto Feast, a small man in the crowd approached me as I came off the stage. He wore a three-piece suit, and a black bowtie. He introduced himself as a music teacher, and offered me a free trip to Italy to study opera with him. At first, I said, 'Okay.' He asked me a few questions, and found out that I liked to drink and also smoked. When he told me I'd have to stop. I said, 'Nah, this is not for me!' Stupidly, I refused a free trip to Italy to study opera. My good times with the guys seemed more important to me at that time."

Just then, Paul, in his usual skeptical manner, kicked in,

"Go, Grandpa. Sing us a song."

Frowning at Paul's mocking tone, my wife encouraged his grandfather, "Go ahead, Charlie. Sing something."

At that moment, without warning, my father's still powerful voice, shattered the air with the opening stanza of a famous tenor aria. All eyes opened wide at the beautiful sound. To Paul's amazement and my delight, my Dad still had it!

After our large meal, including coffee and pastries, the boys and I headed to our basement with Grandpa Charlie for a game of pool. Paul affectionately teased his grandfather when he missed shots and wasn't playing up to his reputation. Now, my wily father had been a semi-pro pool player who dominated pool halls with his inventive games. He would challenge anyone to a pool game, but there was always one condition. It had to be for money, any amount, as long as there was a bet on the table. My father was a lifelong gambler. There was no end to the variety of challenges he concocted. In one of his typical games, a player had to make twenty-five balls to win. But only Charlie, not the other player, had to make the balls consecutively — and one-handed! If he missed the twenty-fourth ball, he had to start over. His talents were limitless, and they weren't confined to the pool table. At one point in his life, he beat a man half his age in a foot race down a city street. His opponent ran normally. Charlie ran backward! There were dozens of similar stories. The odds always seemed irresistible to those who took him on. Most of the time, my sons just rolled their eyes at me, convinced these accounts were completely made up.

After that holiday dinner, my father had to have been annoyed at his grandson's ribbing. Nevertheless, in his customary, good-natured manner, he proposed to all,

"I'll tell you what. Each of you put a dollar on the table as a bet. We will play one rack. Any two of you can take two consecutive shots to my one shot. That's a four-to-one advantage. I have to make ten balls to your five balls. If I lose, I will pay each of you a dollar. Is it a bet?" Paul and his friends were excited and readily agreed. Grandpa Charlie continued,

"Paul, rack 'em up. To make it even better for you, I will break open the rack, and any balls that go into a pocket won't count in my score."

You know the rest of the story. Charlie's five-dollar win went right into David's piggy bank. Both my sons were enriched that night. They discovered my entertaining stories were not just fairy tales.

Those who knew Charlie Beans, as he was called in The BronxLittle Italy neighborhood where I grew up, were familiar with all the stories. His escapades, feats, and foibles were legendary. In good times or bad, in his Mafia-tinged life, he was a neighborhood guy, when neighborhood meant something more than just a group of streets. There were many sides to my father. In his way, he was a stand-up guy, an acclaimed figure they still talk about with awe and affection, generations later. When Beans eventually meets his maker, I wouldn't be surprised if he finds a pool table, a deck of cards, and all the Old Boys from Arthur Avenue waiting for him.

Christmas 1996

Author's Note:

In my father's heyday, no one was walking around with smartphones, ready to take instant photos of the bad, the beautiful, and the unbelievable. Shortly after the Christmas gathering described in the Prologue, I set out to record, in words, some of my father's most memorable and mind-boggling moments. During the process, I wanted to place each of these mini-events in some context, recreating the times and places, as well as the people who inhabited them. Some names have been changed to protect the guilty. Before I knew it, our family history and my own life story came tumbling out.

Neighborhood was everything when I was growing up, and there are many references here to the particular streets and avenues that paved my childhood. I put down the various happenings as I thought of them, and this non-linear memoir is the result. It took awhile, but here now are my father's stories…and mine.

EARLY YEARS

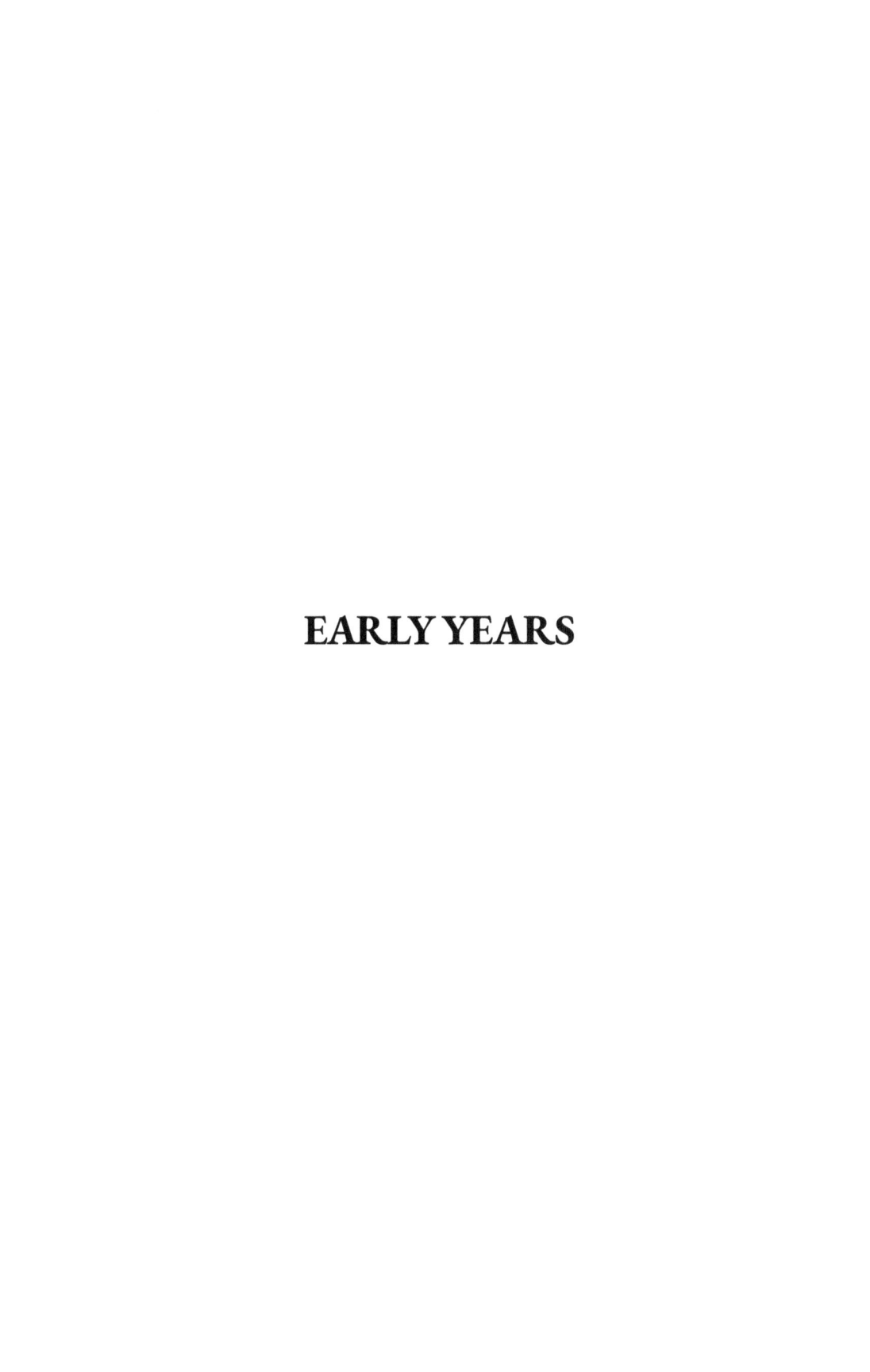

CHAPTER 1

A FOUR-YEAR-OLD'S PERSPECTIVE

On an early autumn afternoon in 1947, in The Bronx neighborhood of my boyhood, a seven-year-old boy took his little brother on a walk through streets without cars that day. My very first memory is this happy one. Festive music often filled the air that week. There were rides, toys, games, and food stands with raw clams on ice, hot Italian food, and delicious pastries. A stage was set up on Periconi Square, featuring local bands and other musical talent. Over the years, I have enjoyed many such warm-weather celebrations, often honoring a particular saint. On this day, my brother Carlo transported me to the wonderland of the San Gennaro festival.

Carlo, age 7

October 14th, that year, started like any other day for me. I was four years old, sitting in my kitchen hideout. The invisible walls of my secret space were framed by four chrome legs. The roof was a Formica tabletop. The day before, Carlo had given me three miniature toy cars as a gift. I finished building my imaginary street, using strips of molding clay as the curbs where I planned to park my little plastic cars. I was busy molding more clay into small bricks to build a garage. I could see my mother's legs carrying her back and forth along the wall that held our kitchen sink and stove. With no wasted energy, she regularly turned to place an object, perhaps a pot of food that was being prepared for dinner, onto the roof of my hideout. My nine-year-old sister, Vita, was in the living room, playing with some of her toys. My younger sister, Barbara, age two, was sleeping in our shared bedroom.

The afternoon sun had passed over our fifth-floor apartment, casting a pleasant ray into the kitchen. I could hear the sing-song chants from the Crystalline Man bouncing off the walls of the courtyard below. This old Italian man was selling laundry bleach to whiten fabrics. Everyone living in an Italian neighborhood at the time had a "crystalline man." My mother gave Vita an order,

"Go get Carlo, and tell him it's time for dinner." There was no reply. A few minutes passed, and again, the order rang out.

"I told you once, and I won't tell you again. Go get Carlo!" This time, Vita jumped up from the couch and answered,

"Okay, okay, I'm putting my shoes on."

The tone of my mother's voice was also a signal that my roadway, garage, automobiles, and hideout would soon have to disappear. Within the next few minutes, life as we knew it would also vanish.

The public hall leading to our apartment was a large open space where the sounds of our neighbors and the smells of their cooking were always present. Most doors to the apartments were kept open when someone was home, especially after school and during holidays. Music from radios, children playing, neighbors talking, and family arguments would echo from the hall. No concern for privacy existed. We were, in a sense, one extended family, and the large hall on our floor served as a kind of communal living room for all. Vita had just stepped into the kitchen on her way to get Carlo when suddenly, an eruption of cries, screams, and shouts reverberated through our apartment. Frightened, I froze under the table as I watched sets of legs draped in aprons and house dresses enter our kitchen. Crying, my mother's closest friend and neighbor, Ann Fusco, reached out for my mother, and I heard,

"Sylvia, Carlo was hit by a car."

My mother fainted before my eyes. At this moment, no one in the room knew my brother had been killed instantly.   I don't know how I got up there, but I definitely remember Maria Colabella's hands firmly pressing down on my thighs, supporting me as I sat on the edge of the kitchen table. Our kitchen was large for a four-room apartment. The table kept shaking from people bumping into it. It had been pushed up against the wall to make more room for neighbors coming and going. There was hardly any room to move. The unfamiliar position I was in, allowing me to look at grown-ups at eye level, distracted me. All I could see were the heads and shoulders of neighbors and friends who were rapidly filling our home to comfort my family. The air was filled with talking, sobbing, and moaning. Commotion was everywhere. Bewildered and curious, I kept turning left and right, and each time I tried to twist myself around to see more, Maria would gently stop me. Suddenly, like a cannon going off, the front door to our apartment slammed shut so hard and loud that the walls shook. I heard someone's hurried footsteps rushing down our long front hall, coming to an abrupt halt when met by the crowd at the entrance to the kitchen. There stood a riveting presence. It was my father, known to most as Charlie Beans. Dressed in a dark blue camel hair overcoat over a business suit, he looked to me like a man in command. He moved forward decisively, parting the crowd, pushing his way past me into the living room where my mother was seated. At this moment, the impressive man in the blue coat, with tears in his eyes, was nothing more than an ordinary father overcome with grief at losing his first-born son. The frightened and confused four-year-old perched on the edge of the kitchen table, did not yet know how profoundly this horrific event would impact his family and his life. The tragic death of my brother Carlo altered the blueprint of all our lives, forever. Gone was any sense of belonging, stability, and family love the three remaining Lucido children had enjoyed while living at 187th Street.

In the coming months, one diversion for Vita and me was the long Saturday afternoon matinee devoted to children's features at Cinelli's Italian-American Savoy movie theatre. Popularly known as The Dumps, the place was located about four blocks from where we lived. Vita would take me there and, on the way, buy us a bagful of Lupini beans for a nickel. The store owner would scoop them out from a barrel of wet beans, dry them, and fill a paper bag for us. While watching the movies, we would squeeze the flat ends and pop the tasty bean into our mouths, littering the floor beneath our seats with the outer skins. We'd be there for about three hours, arriving at noon to watch cartoons, comedy shorts, a movie, and finally, the special on-screen car races. Each movie ticket came with a car number on it, and any kid holding a winning number would receive a small toy as a prize. I was always one of the winners! For some unknown reason, the ticket lady always winked at me and handed me a winning ticket. I shared my prizes with both my sisters.

As time went on, my friendships with the children of my age in our building was another source of comfort for me. I still have a clear memory of the cold winter mornings. I walked down the floor flights of stairs, collecting the other five kindergarteners until we reached the last one, Annamarie Angrasanni. Her mother, Carmela, had ready for each of us a shot glass with a dash of Scotch to warm us up before we walked across 187th Street and up Beaumont Avenue Hill to PS 32 at 183rd Street. It never occurred to me that I was passing the fateful spot that claimed my brother's life.

In 1947, my father was the wealthiest man living at 707 East 187th Street. He had income from three ten-seat barber shops in Manhattan.

We were the first family to have a TV set in our building. The previous Christmas, he bought us kids many things, including a mini-electric pinball machine, toy guns, dolls, and assorted other toys. He gave Carlo a shiny red, two-wheeled scooter. It was his pride and joy, but my mother was upset that my father gave him that gift. Not wanting him riding around in the streets, she chained it to a railing attached to the coal chute in the basement of our building. That didn't faze my brother. Like other kids in the neighborhood, he built his own.

But it wasn't very long after Carlo's death that the cracks in our family life began to show. Hanging out with the wrong group of people, my father carelessly spent money at the racetrack and in nightclubs and caroused with women, neglecting his wife and children. He ignored the businesses he successfully built up over the years, resulting in the gradual loss of all three barber shops. Slowly, he regressed to the kind of lifestyle he had at a much earlier time when he ran errands for the Mafia while living in Italian East Harlem.

CHAPTER 2

CHARLIE BEANS

Born Biagio Lucido in the old country, Sicily, my father's name was Americanized to Charles on the ship's manifest. He emigrated to America as a seven-year-old, in 1919. His father, Francesco, known to us as Grandpa Frank, opened a barber shop on New York City's Lower East Side, on Avenue B and East Tenth Street. As a young boy, my father worked there after school, sweeping the floor and cleaning the counters and chairs. The family lived behind the shop in a very small apartment.

Dad told me just one story about those early years. Once a month, the local policeman who pounded that beat would come to the shop for his usual free shave and haircut. He dressed in an impressive blue uniform with ten shiny brass buttons and never removed his jacket. In those days, the New York City police force was mostly Irish. The cops in the neighborhood made sure the local businesses toed the line. Some took advantage of recent immigrants, especially those still learning English. Sicilians, in particular, had a built-in suspicion of authority and understood the unspoken language of graft. They went along with it to avoid abuse or harm.

One day, after school, young Charlie came into the shop with a deep cut on his forehead, bleeding badly. Grandpa Frank's first reaction was anger. Normally a quiet man, he raised his voice, asking in broken English,

"How did this happen? Who did this to you?"

"I was in a fight with some kids."

"In a fight?" What did they hit you with, a rock? You're

"No, they didn't hit me. The policeman hit me with his club."

Grandpa Frank

"Policeman! What policeman?"

"You know, the cop who comes in here all the time."

My grandfather closed the shop and took his son to the hospital. A few weeks later, the boy was doing his usual after-school chores when the policeman made his regular visit to the shop and sat right down in his usual chair. Grandpa Frank tilted the chair back, placing a short barber's towel under the man's neck instead of draping him with the usual barber's cape. He mixed shaving soap with a horsehair brush and lathered one side of the policeman's face. My father's memory of the incident was razor-sharp. His father held two straight razors, one in each hand. Standing behind the police officer, he began the motion of a shave with his left hand, but lower down, placing the other razor at the policeman's neck. Raising his right hand above the cop's chest, he motioned his son to stand in front of the man, addressing the officer in the unmistakable accent of Sicily,

"You know who this boy is?" As young Charlie watched in disbelief, with a flick of his right hand, Grandpa sliced off one of the brass buttons from the cop's jacket. It went flying into the air, landing with a ping on the floor next to my father. Terrified, the cop stuttered in his heavy Irish accent,

"Yes, he's your s-s...son."

I hung on to Dad's every word, waiting to hear what came next. He described how Grandpa swiftly sliced a second button from the cop's jacket. Its loud clinking, as it bounced rhythmically along the hard tile floor in the now deadly silent room, added to the intense sense of danger.

"You know he's my boy. You see the patch on his head? You did this to my son!" Now shaking, his voice quivering, the cop responded,

"Yes, I'm very sorry. I didn't realize it was your son! I just saw some boys fighting. Please! I'm sorry!"

Dispatching a third button, my grandfather voiced unequivocally,

"If you ever step in my shop again, I will slice your neck from ear to ear. And I warn you, now. No, I promise you — if you try to hurt my family or me, your life will not be spared. Do you understand me?"

It was not an empty threat. Although he was no longer associated with the Sicilian Mafia, Grandpa had powerful mob friends, including family, in Manhattan and Brooklyn, who helped him when he arrived in New York. Neither that police officer nor any other ever again set foot in my grandfather's barber shop.

Some years later, when the family moved to Italian East Harlem, my father was given his nickname, "Beans," which stuck with him for the rest of his life. As a teenager, he often delivered messages for the Mafia. An oral message was the only permissible method of communication between those guys. One day, he was sent to a club on 116th Street and Pleasant Avenue to find a mob figure, "Mr. Dreams." Entering, he asked if "Mr. Beans" was in. The men there burst out laughing and found it so funny that from that day on, every time Dad visited such hangouts, they would call out, "Hey, Beans! How ya doing?"

My father's life was a treasure trove of colorful stories that people loved to tell about him. Some he recounted to me, himself, in a very matter-of-fact way. Some I heard from others. One or two incidents I witnessed myself. To many, Charlie Beans was the most unforgettable character they'd ever met.

An East Harlem Rival

Once, after seeing a John Wayne movie with my father, he casually mentioned he had known another famous film star of the era. At age sixteen, he sometimes hung out on the streets with fellow teenagers and East Harlem neighbor Burt Lancaster. In 1929, Dad was an excellent athlete but not in the same league as Lancaster. He repeatedly fell grossly short of every challenge with Lancaster in any sport. One day, after school, they found themselves in a narrow alleyway between two buildings. There was enough space for each of them to rest his back against one building wall while wedging his feet against the opposite wall. They both got into position and, using their feet, began to inch themselves upward between the two walls. When they'd almost reached the second floor of the building, Lancaster gave up, saying,

"I'm not going any further." My father, now at the brink of his very first victory over his nemesis, ignored him and kept moving, calling to him to catch up. Lancaster told him he'd had enough, freed his legs from the wall, and dropped safely to the ground. Charlie quickly realized he'd made a dangerous mistake. He was too high above the ground. The only way down was to release his legs and drop. But If he did so, he would likely break his legs or worse. He thought he was going to die! The only possible way to save himself was to continue wedging his body up the building's remaining four floors to the safety of the roof — which he proceeded to do, inch by inch, heart in his mouth, the whole time.

"Thank God, there was a steel railing I could grasp and pull myself up onto the roof behind me. Otherwise, I would not be here today telling you this story." He told me he was incredibly lucky that the railing was there instead of the usual parapet wall at the top. Once he knew he was safe, he managed to walk down the five flights to the street.

What Will He Think of Next?

Cool under fire, Charlie remained something of a daredevil all of his life. His future escapades largely took place in The Bronx. When my family lived there, our Arthur Avenue section was one of several Italian-American enclaves in the borough. It was called Fordham by most residents, not Belmont, as some refer to it today. At the time, the neighborhood male population had many social activities and gathering places. There were blue-collar workers who enjoyed espresso, bocce, and a trick-taking Italian card game called Briscola. A smaller group of guys were good-timers and entrepreneurs who liked to party and were always ready for some *grappa* and a poker game. And then there were the "wise guys," the Mafia members who lived and worked in the neighborhood and regularly showed up at local functions.

Storefronts, bars, grills, and social clubs were the most popular places where men would meet, often cooking up money-making schemes, some legal, some not so legal, for themselves and for others who might be interested in cashing in on so-called good deals. In the late 1940s, in one such watering hole, George's Bar and Grill, my sister Vita and I saw our father jump over a bar stool to win a bet.

It was an extraordinary sight. To the wondering eyes of all onlookers, *from a standing position*, he leaped high in the air, effortlessly clearing the stool to land on the other side. Early on, he had gained a reputation as a gifted athlete by performing jaw-dropping feats that you'd never find in the sports columns. Stunts like catching chestnuts in his mouth that had been tossed down to him from the roof of a five-story building. Or using a broom handle like a golf club to hit stones aimed at breaking a milk bottle hung on the wall of a handball court. Or, even more spectacularly, pole vaulting from the street into the window of Pop's poolroom! All these performances by Charlie Beans were designed for the sole purpose of winning bets. George's Bar and Grill, across the street from our home, was a frequent stop before Sunday dinners. On one occasion, it was almost 3 pm and time to break for dinner when Beans proposed a new bet for the following Sunday. It would take place along the two unbroken blocks of Crotona Avenue between 187th and 189th Streets.

"I'll tell you what. I will race anyone in the neighborhood. I will run backward, and they can run forward as long as I get some kind of head start."

"Yeah, sure. You run twenty feet, and we run more than a block," scoffed one of the guys.

"No, seriously, just give me a reasonable head start. Let's say," pausing deliberately, as if the idea had just struck him, "I start running backward from in front of Delaboves's building; one of you guys starts from Silvio's Bar. The first to get to 189th Street wins the race."

"Are you serious, Charlie?"

"Yes! Is it a bet?"

Guys were shaking their heads. Charlie Beans thinks he's going to win another crazy bet. But racing someone backward? C'mon! The word went out, and bookies began banking bets. There was no problem finding neighborhood athletes to take him up on the challenge. One stepped up, and the race was on. Beans was nobody's fool. Weeks earlier, stopwatch in hand, my father secretly ran forward at top speed from Silvio's bar at Crotona Avenue and 187th Street, the two unbroken blocks to 189th Street. He then tested himself running backward, starting from various locations along the same route. He calculated that he, who was the fastest runner in the neighborhood, could not beat himself running forward from Silvio's if he started backward at or near Delabove's apartment building. The rest of the story is Fordham's history. Beans cleaned up. Big time!

CHAPTER 3

SOUTHERN BOULEVARD

Four years had passed since my brother's death. Unemployed, my father was going from job to job. We were now living in a small two-bedroom apartment on the third floor of a five-story walk-up in the South Bronx. My parents' relationship was, to say the least, strained. To help support the family, my mother found work cleaning offices in a nearby professional building.

The elevated IRT train, popularly known as the "El," was no more than twenty- five feet away, directly across from our apartment at 174th Street and Southern Boulevard. I could have thrown a ball straight out our living room window and easily hit a passing train. In the next building lived my mother's elderly aunt, Zizi. We thought she was our grandmother, not knowing that "Zizi" probably derived from *Zia,* the Italian word for aunt. She was Marcella Donisi Marconi, my grandfather Achille Donisi's sister.

Zizi had no children and cared for us as if we were her own. All smiles as she greeted us. I can still picture her in her house dress, with an apron tied at her neck and waist and her gray hair neatly rolled into a bun. She was especially attentive to me. She would often run her hand over my hair, clasp my face in her two hands, and kiss me on the forehead, whispering, *"Io amo il mio bambino."* ("I love you, my baby.")

In all kinds of weather, my two sisters and I would walk the long three-and-a-half blocks to and from PS 50 on Vyse Avenue. Although the school served free lunch for those in need, my mother would not allow us to accept charity. Instead, we would walk back to Southern Boulevard and quickly climb the six flights to Zizi's apartment for our midday meal. We were afraid of her husband, Tony Marconi, a mean, unhappy man who never recovered from being swindled by developers of valuable property he owned that ran along The Bronx River. Masking his cruelty as affection, he often used his

My sisters, Vita and Barbara, with me

fingers to flick the back of our heads with a heavy hand. Obediently, the three of us would seat ourselves on the wooden bench that rested against the wall facing the kitchen table. We watched Zizi carefully cut thin slices of Italian bread from a large round loaf. With her left hand cradling the loaf of bread close to her breast and using her right hand like a violinist, she skillfully slid the long knife back and forth through the bread. The knife made its way through the crackling crust until perfectly even slices floated onto the table. This ritual was a beautiful sight that always warmed my heart. Our favorite lunch was a slice of bread with a hole cut in the center, pan-toasted in a thin coat of olive oil in a heavy black iron frying pan. Zizi would brown one side of the bread, then turn it over and toast the other side before cracking an egg into the hole in the middle. As an adult, I've re-created this comfort food countless times.

Charles Lucido, a.k.a Charlie Beans

My First Adventure

In the summer of 1951, my father found employment as a barber in Edgemere, Far Rockaway, one of the beach communities within sight and smell of the ocean, favored by New York City dwellers. He lived on Beach 34th Street in a room above a fish store, across the street from the barbershop.

I was eight years old and about to embark on the first adventure of my young life. Like most kids in my Bronx neighborhood, I was used to getting around on my own and often took short trolley rides by myself. I had never been on a train before, but my mother allowed me to take the El all by myself from 174th Street to stay with my father for a few weeks. In retrospect, it amazes me that my mother permitted me to take that solo trip.

It was a wonderful, above-ground two-hour trip. Crossing the Third Avenue Bridge into Manhattan, then the much larger Manhattan Bridge into Brooklyn and Queens, I saw many different neighborhoods. This was my first glimpse of a world beyond The Bronx! I can still feel the clacking rhythm of the train under my feet as I moved from one side of the car to the other to catch the changing views. This was unbelievably exciting!

Beyond Broad Channel Island, Far Rockaway was waiting for me. Changing trains when needed, I arrived at Beach 36th Street-Edgemere,

Me at age 10

carrying my light bag of clothing. I carefully checked the last instruction on my mother's note, which is now very wrinkled in my pocket. I had only a short walk to the barbershop.

The next few weeks were full of new sights, sounds, and sensations. I was allowed to go to the beach whenever I wanted. I became friends with some older kids who were summer vacationers. New to the ocean and not yet knowing how to swim, I stayed close to the shore, never venturing beyond where the waves broke at my knees. It was fabulous! One day, while hanging out on the boardwalk, eleven-year-old Naomi, one of my new friends, invited me to her birthday party. At the party, she coaxed me to dance for the first time in my life. Shy at first, I danced with her several times! After the second dance, I needed no more inducement. The scent of her hairspray was enough for me to fall in love.

During that summer, my mother's sister, Anna LoCicero, rented a roomy bungalow for her family a short walk from where my father was living. She invited my mother and sisters to come for a week's stay with them. During that time, my family was together again, and both the Lucidos and LoCiceros had a great time together. It was then that I formed a lifelong friendship with my cousin Mario, who was a teenager at the time. He took me to the boardwalk several times, where we had fun riding the carousel, driving the bumper cars, and playing games of chance — as well as consuming lots of frankfurters and cotton candy. That week was one of my all-time happiest childhood memories.

Clarence Williams

The neighborhood around Southern Boulevard was changing. Puerto Ricans and Blacks were settling in all around the South Bronx. The residents on this street were predominantly of European extraction: Germans, Italians, Irish and Jewish. The only Black people on my street were the superintendent of our building, Mr. Williams, and his wife and family, who lived in the basement apartment. Their younger son, Clarence, became a close friend and protector of my sisters and me. The changing cultures in the neighborhood brought tension to our school. Clarence, who was my age, towered over most of the kids in our grade. He was a leader among the Black kids. There were threatening groups of all kinds ready to start trouble. When my sisters and I left school for lunch, we had to leave the schoolyard on Bryant Avenue. This way, the Principal could keep an eye on all these groups, making sure all students left the premises at the same time, from the same exit. On days when tensions were stirring, Clarence and a friend of his would meet us in the schoolyard and walk us to 173rd Street, where there was no risk of trouble. Most days, we would all walk home together. He made sure no one harmed us.

My mother didn't want me to play with Clarence. At age thirteen, she had been placed in an orphanage, where she had some run-ins with Black children that made her instinctively wary of colored people. These unhappy experiences left an indelible mark. However, I clearly remember Mom once scolding me when she heard me call the superintendent of our building on 187th Street by his first name. She told me the super, a Black man, was a married man with two children and was to be addressed as Mr. Crawford.

One day, Mom overheard Vita telling me to make up with Clarence after we had a pushing fight to make sure there were no hard feelings. Hearing this, my mother, sometimes a fiery, irrational woman, ordered me to "Go kick his ass!" Black or white, it didn't make a difference. Her son had to stand his ground. She insisted that I show him I was no pushover. The next day, on our way home, Vita and I told Clarence what my mother said. Laughing, he replied,

"You don't want to fight me, do you?"

"Of course not! Do I want to wind up in a hospital? You'll murder me. My mother is crazy!"

"I don't want to fight you either. We're friends."

"Clarence, my mother expects me to fight you. Let's do this. I will tell her we will fight in my yard after school tomorrow. I know she will be looking out the window when we get home. Both of us go into the alleyway leading to my backyard. Hang out there for a few minutes, maybe play some handball. Then I will leave alone and go home. I'll tell her we fought and then made up after. What do you think?"

Laughing along with Vita, Clarence replied,

"Sounds good to me. Are all Italians crazy?"

Later, when my sisters and I told my mother how good a friend Clarance was to us, she told me to bring him to our apartment so she could meet him. I remember the uneasy look on her face the afternoon he came into the kitchen where she was preparing dinner. He brought to mind the unpleasant memories of her childhood. I believe that Clarence's visit and his kindness to her children opened her eyes to her knee-jerk suspicion of

African Americans. Clarence was welcome in our home after that. I learned from her example that people can change when they have a good reason to change.

Clarence and I became fast friends. Along with other kids on the block, we played the popular street games of the times — spinning tops, shooting marbles, stoop ball, Hit the Stick, box ball, and Ring-a-levIo. During the summers, I often had lunch at his home after playing ball in our backyard. His mother often made delicious collard greens with some fried fish. This seemed strange to me, as my family cooked fish only on Fridays. Some nine years later, I was able, in a small way, to repay Clarence for his kindness.

CHAPTER 4

EDDIE THE CARPENTER

In the early fall of 1952, I noticed a new tenant in the formerly vacant store at the front of my building. Every day, from then on, from one corner of the store window, I would peek into the place. The strange-looking man inside worked all alone. I say strange because I had never before seen anyone with *Alopecia areata,* or "spot baldness," as it is commonly known. This very quiet, homely man was strongly built. His pale face was speckled with large, unsightly freckles, and his old-fashioned wire-rimmed eyeglasses did nothing to improve his appearance. His head was mostly bald and dotted all over with small sections of hair, which made him look even worse. He had a sad and lonely look. Some of the kids would throw old bottle caps and marbles at his window.

    The weeks went by, and I could see the man wasn't making much headway. I became curious about the kind of store he was setting up. The inside was no more than 16 x 40 feet. As the days and weeks passed, I never failed to check on his progress. I was watching a carpenter's shop emerge. Visible on the right side was a long workbench with a vice and a few tools. Others hung haphazardly from hooks on the wall above the bench. In the center of the shop stood an impressive new steel bench saw. Unknown to this nine-year-old, this particular bench would have been in my life for decades. I could see this carpenter didn't have much work. Most of the time, he sat reading a newspaper. Months went by, and every day, I would gravitate to the same corner of the window to watch what he was doing, many times foregoing playing with my friends. I was fascinated, watching him work hard to make simple repairs on furniture or struggling to build small bookcases. During warm weather, when he was not working in his shop, he would sit outside reading the New York Post or a book. Most of the time, if kids came near him, he would quietly pick up his chair and go back inside. I thought he didn't like children, especially the ones who taunted him. I felt that he looked at me differently, maybe because he'd noticed that I seemed to enjoy watching him work from a distance. Years later, I learned he was aware his appearance disturbed people and didn't want to frighten anyone.

One quiet afternoon, the carpenter was working in the rear of his shop. I was flipping baseball cards with a couple of friends in front of the building when a boy about our age came walking past us with a terribly contorted hobble. At the time, I knew nothing about cerebral palsy. Making his way, minding his own business, he was followed by two of my other neighborhood friends. They were imitating his broken movements, mocking him, encouraging others to taunt him. When they came near me, I was so disturbed by what they were doing that I called out to them to leave the boy alone. They ignored me.

I picked up the carpenter's chair and ran ahead of them, placing myself between the boy and my two friends. Using the chair as a barrier, I yelled out to them to stop it and leave him alone. Irritated at my interference, they gave an obscene hand gesture and retreated. Meanwhile, the carpenter had come out of his shop and observed the tormentors and the scene that unfolded. As I replaced the chair and hurried to catch up with the boy to accompany him to the end of the block, the carpenter and I made eye contact for the first time. Walking back, I found him sitting in the chair. As I was about to pass him, he waved a dollar bill in his hand, softly calling me.

"Sonny, would you please go around the corner and get me a container of coffee?" I was surprised at the kind voice that emerged from this scary-looking man.

"Sure."

He handed me the dollar and told me to get a candy bar or soda for myself. When I returned with his coffee, he was inside the shop. I stopped at the doorway and called out to him,

"Mister, I have your coffee."

"Come in, son. Did you get something for yourself?"

"Yes, I got a Babe Ruth bar."

"That's good. My name is Eddie. What's yours?"

I told him my name. I had just met the man who would become my mentor, my friend, and a benevolent influence throughout my life. From this time on, I spent many of my after-school hours in his shop. I would help him by holding one end of a cabinet as he drove a nail into the other end, or by fetching nails or a screwdriver, or by simply getting him a cup of coffee from around the corner. My mother knew how friendly I was with Eddie. One night after dinner, she questioned me closely about him and then asked if he ever touched me. Realizing what she was getting at, I assured her he had never laid a finger on me. I was afraid she might cause an end to this new friendship until several days before Christmas when I found a package on my bed, neatly wrapped in brown paper tied with a string. She had added a note, "To Eddie, from Frank." I brought the package to my mother and asked,

"Mom, is this a Christmas present for Eddie?" She smiled and said,

"Yes, Frank, it's for your friend. You give it to him for Christmas. It's a carton of cigarettes." I believe my mother saw in Eddie a positive paternal quality, constant and stable, that was missing in my life at the time.

In the summers that followed, and for many years after, I happily served as Eddie's helper and became educated in a useful trade. He owned a 1948 Chevrolet station wagon that had beautiful solid wood trim, an appropriate look for a carpenter's car. He used the car not only for his business but also to drive vacationers to bungalows in the Catskills to help make a day's pay. Soon, he was making carpentry repairs in the neighborhood and later throughout The Bronx and Manhattan, with the help of some skilled employees. He was finally making a decent living, and I was working regularly, both with him and part-time, for my father.

Eddie's Father

Eddie's father came into my life when I was in my mid-teens. He was a Russian immigrant who always looked disgruntled. He had just given up his shop on Claremont Parkway after a high rent increase. Ben Borkowsky was an old-school European cabinet maker. By watching him closely, I learned how to make tongue and groove corners and mitered edges. Even the parts no one could see were finished beautifully. This was my introduction to professionally made cabinetry.

A big man with a deep bass voice, he was an intimidating presence. At first, he ignored me as if I didn't exist. He was reluctant to teach me anything, and I tried to stay out of his way. A time came when he was wrestling a long piece of lumber, trying to cut it. He needed help. Knowing he wouldn't seek my assistance unsolicited, I grabbed one end of the board firmly and secured it in such a way as to keep it from splitting. He was impressed with the skill I had shown, and from then on, I became his helper in the shop. Mr. Borkowsky now made sure the shop was kept neat and clean in order to perform his trade efficiently. He brought in new business for Eddie by displaying his well-made cabinetry in the shop window. This arrangement worked out well for both father and son.

Some months later, Eddie had a job for me on Isham Street in upper Manhattan. Leaving the shop entrusted to his father, he drove me to the job site, a five-story walk-up, while he went to look at a few potential jobs nearby. My work was on the top floor. In one trip, I managed to make my way up all five flights, carrying wood strips and a toolbox in my right hand while my left hand awkwardly balanced a pair of double-hung windows against my left shoulder.

About an hour later, I finished installing the new windows and worked in the hall to repair the defective door jamb using the new wood strips. The door to this apartment was near an ornate railing where I could see anyone coming up to the fifth floor. After working in that drab apartment, I was invigorated by the sun beaming down from the skylight above my work area and on the stairs below. I heard the slow shuffling of feet laboriously climbing up the stairway. Floor by floor, the sound got progressively louder until I saw it came from Eddie. I knew something was wrong.

Eddie never dragged his feet. He was always rushing someplace. I stopped what I was doing, put my hammer and chisel down, and went to greet him. Maybe he hurt himself? Holding tightly onto the banister, step by step, he wearily approached the landing, his head bowed. He looked as if he was in pain.

"Eddie, are you all right? Are you hurt?"

He raised his head and looked at me with glistening eyes.

"Frank, my father hung himself in the shop."

The first and only time in my life I ever embraced Eddie was on that day, on those stairs, in upper Manhattan.

Life Goes On

Eddie frequently encouraged me to further my education. Repairing floors and doors for now was okay, but I must aim higher. Also, he saw I was not on the right track with the goings-on in my father's club. This self-educated man didn't let a day go by without teaching me something. To get to our jobs, we often drove along the Grand Concourse, a street that ran the length of The Bronx and was lined with expensive Art Deco buildings. He often stopped by different apartment houses to show me their magnificent lobbies and describe the architecture. He was proud that the elegant long expanse of the Grand Concourse was in The Bronx and that it was modeled on the Champs-Élysées in Paris.

I'll never forget the day we were driving north on the Concourse and stopped at a light on 161st Street at The Bronx courthouse. My eyes were fixed on two men crossing the street. One was dressed in work clothes, the other in a suit. I watched them reach the other side of the street when the light changed. At the next stoplight, Eddie broke the silence in the car with a question. He asked me about the two men I had been watching.

"Frank, what was the difference between the two men that you just saw crossing 161st Street?" I thought for a while and replied,

"The man in the suit looked like a rich man. The other man looked poor."

"No, Frank, the difference between the two men was the man with the suit had an education. The man in work clothes didn't."

By 1960, I had a part-time job as his apprentice and was also working with my father in his new business venture. One memorable hot August day, a week before my seventeenth birthday, Eddie had an emergency call to replace a basement staircase in The Bronx. It was in a dark, dimly lit cellar. Having a prior appointment, he worked feverishly to get the job done. Sweat ran down his face, tripping on his scattered tools, and he made incorrect cuts in the staircase stringer and other costly mistakes. He was getting nowhere, and I finally had to say something.

"Eddie, you're rushing, and you're going to hurt yourself. Why not let me work here, and you go look at the other job?"

"Frank, do you think you can do this job alone? It's a lot of work."

"Sure I can, Eddie. Let me do the job. You go. Don't worry, I can do this!"

"Okay, Frank. I will be back in an hour to finish up."

When he returned, he found me sitting on the next-to-last step of the new staircase I built. The work area was cleaned up, and all the tools were neatly stowed in his toolbox. Standing there, with a look of amazement, he studied the job. Softly, he said,

"Frank, today the boy became the teacher. The man became the student.

LIFE BEYOND THE BRONX

CHAPTER 5

COUNTRY LIVING

In the early 1950s, looking for work, my father followed the summer barbering trade to the resort community in Monticello, New York. He arranged for a real family vacation for the first time. Getting to know many influential year-round residents, he was persuaded to think about relocating to the area. Originally home to Jewish landowners and farmers who rented out rooms to vacationers, the area eventually caught on and became a popular summer getaway. It became known as the Borscht Belt or Jewish Alps. Thousands of holiday-seekers, mostly Jewish New Yorkers from all five boroughs of the city, as well as from nearby New Jersey, would fill the hundreds of bungalow colonies and hotels. Hotels like The Concord, Grossinger's, Brown's Hotel, The Raleigh, and dozens of others became famous for their sumptuous meals, special weekends for Singles, and for featuring top Jewish entertainers like Jerry Lewis, George Burns, Jack Benny, Mel Brooks, Barbara Streisand, and many other big stars like Tony Bennett, Dean Martin, and Sammy Davis, Jr.

Eager to leave the city behind him and start a new life for the family, my father rented the entire top floor of a two-family house in the rural town of Ferndale, eleven miles north of Monticello. With the help of his new local friends, he was able to secure a job in Liberty, just three miles north of Ferndale.

No more noisy trains rumbling past my window. I no longer had to share a bed with my two sisters. Each of us had our newly-furnished room. In addition to the four bedrooms, our family's large, self-contained apartment included a living room, sunroom, and a kitchen of our own. We were in the country! Fields, rivers, and woodlands surrounded us. Our Ferndale home was on Rural Route 17. We didn't even have a mailbox. Seeing the need for a bicycle, my father bought me my first and only bike. It was a three-speed English racer that I cherished! One of my chores was to walk or cycle a mile and a half to pick up our mail at the general store, which also served as the local post office.

The store's postal clerk sorted the mail and placed it in the P.O. Boxes that lined one wall. This new life suited my father and all of us.

A year later, Dad opened his barbershop. It was in an excellent location, across the street from the bus terminal where most of the summer people arrived. His shop had a traditional, rotating red-and-white, diagonally striped barber pole on the outside and three barber chairs inside. One chair was for him, and one for a second full-time barber he employed. The third would be used by an extra barber, who would be hired during the busy season.

My dad would distract frightened children by singing silly ditties to them, in time to the clicking of his scissors as he snipped their hair. When he worked on adults, the popular songs he sang in his beautiful tenor voice reached the street and drew customers into his shop. A sizable number of his clientele were Orthodox Jews who began coming to the shop, enjoying his good spirits and his extensive repertoire of Yiddish expressions. He would greet them with Bagrisung and *bite zitsn*. (Welcome, please be seated.)

It was 1954. My sisters helped our mother at home and also had their own Ferndale friends. During the summer months, I liked spending time in the barber shop, doing odd jobs for my father. When I wasn't running errands or sweeping the floor, I occupied myself at a small table in the back by drawing images of the place and practicing three-dimensional lettering. My pictures were neatly displayed at the haircutting stations for customers to see. One of the Jewish men particularly liked my 3-D work and told my father he would pay me three dollars to make a big birthday sign for him in Hebrew.

Later in the summer, when Dad's business slowed down, I had a part-time job, earning ten cents a game as a pin boy in the bowling alley a few blocks away. It was dangerous work, but at that young age, I felt very grown up, having a paying job.

Pin boys worked in a dingy, smelly, unclean place. We had to move fast to avoid being caught in the motorized pin-setting machinery. Jumping in and out of a five-foot deep, four-foot square space was definitely hazardous, and the possibility of being hit by a flying bowling pin that a 17mph speeding bowling ball had struck was always present. My father showed no interest in my working conditions or whether the owner paid any attention to child labor laws. I soon became proficient enough to handle three alleys at a time, occasionally working five hours straight, earning as much as ten dollars in one afternoon.

Early one summer morning, my mother heard someone knocking at our front door and went to answer it. She called up to me,

"Frankie, there's someone here to see you."

Springing up from my bed, I ran to the foot of the stairs to see who would be visiting me so early. I was amazed to see Eddie the Carpenter standing there. The night before, he had driven his sisters to a bungalow colony in Monticello. Wanting me to enjoy Eddie's visit without my sisters disturbing us, Mom quietly made breakfast just for us. As I was leaving to take Eddie to the barber shop, she reminded me to show him the tree house I built with a neighbor behind our house. My father was happy to see Eddie, too. He told me to show him the town and asked him to stay for dinner. Eddie declined because he was committed to being with his sisters on their first night in the country. Before we returned to Ferndale, I took him to the bowling alley where I worked. One of the pin boys let me pin a couple of games to show off my skills. Eddie was really impressed but cautioned me that this was a dangerous job.

Horace Duncombe

My school was in Liberty, north of Ferndale. I soon made a new friend, Horace Duncombe, another transplanted student. Like me, he could not meet the reading requirements and had to repeat the fifth grade. He was a Black kid, and we became close friends. Most of the kids in Liberty were nice. By default, we hung out with the few troublemakers.

For my birthday that year, I received a reversible red and tan jacket. At lunchtime one school day, in the fall, Horace and I were headed back from the baseball field when a rock, thrown by one of the other kids, crashed through one of the school windows.

Everyone started running in different directions. A teacher stepping out a door yelled to me to stop. Afraid he would blame me, I ran as fast as I could. He came running after me, but I had a good head start, and when I turned the corner of the building, I ran up a nearby stairway into the school. Instinctively, I unzipped my jacked, turned it inside out to the red side, re-zipped it, and casually walked back out the way I had come in. There, coming around the corner, was the teacher. Out of breath, he asked me if I'd seen a boy run by in a tan jacket. Without batting an eye, I calmly replied,

"I just came from the lunchroom. I didn't see anybody." He continued straight ahead, searching for the rock thrower. For how long, I didn't wait to see. I walked back to the schoolyard, where I met up with Horace. He never mentioned the change in the color of my jacket.

Thank You, Grace Van Dyck

I played outdoor games with the local kids, like touch football, badminton, and hide and seek. When we played hide and seek, Grace Van Dyck, one of the Free Methodist girls made it a point to hide with me. I thought this was to avoid being near certain rude or rough boys. Her angelic face and shy way befitted a girl from a religious background. One late afternoon, we were hiding in the second level of a rickety, makeshift tree house near the woods behind my house. One of the kids saw us through the hut's small window. We were caught and had to surrender. Going up into the tree hut was easier than coming down. I told Grace I would go first, just in case she fell. We reached the lower level safely. To continue past this level, we had to raise a trap door on the floor and then climb down a seven-foot ladder. Turning myself around to climb down the ladder, I had to face Grace. To my amazement, suddenly, she kissed me on the cheek. A flow of emotions came over me — jitters, shock, fright, confusion, happiness, elation. Was this to be my first girlfriend? While on a brief stay with my father in Far Rockaway, I had my first blissful experience with the fair sex. My friendship with Grace blossomed into a sensual delight, exposing me to a new part of life.

Our second-floor Ferndale home

My drawing at age 13 years old

CHAPTER 6

HUGH HICKS AND "MR. CHARLIE"

The spring of 1952 was nearing. Dad was doing well in his new barber shop. My family was happily intact, enjoying our new life in the country. An unemployed Black man took a job with a private taxi service, driving New Yorkers to Monticello and other towns in the Catskills. One of his drop-off points was in Liberty, New York. He had time to kill before his trip back. Wandering around the town, he was especially interested in the turn-of-the-century building that housed the bowling alleys and poolroom. He liked what he saw and figured, being down on his luck, he had nothing to lose: He made a decision — he was going to make his home in Liberty. He rented a room and went back to the city. Returning soon by bus to his new hometown, he was dropped off at the Short Line Bus terminal across the street from my father's barbershop. Walking past the shop, he heard my father singing and stopped to listen. Seeing him outside, Dad stepped away from his chair and went to the open door. In a low voice, he said,

"I cut *everyone's* hair. Do you need a haircut?"

"Oh, no, sir, I was just admiring your voice."

"Well, when you come in, I'll sing for you, too!"

At this time, most barbers wouldn't cut the hair of Black men, claiming it was too thick, and would dull their scissors. This man felt a ray of hope. A kind person? Maybe he had made the right decision. When about a week had passed, he was settled in his room and made it livable, but he was still unable to find work. Anxiously, a bold Idea came to him. He walked down to see the Singing Barber.

It was Saturday, usually the busiest day of the week, but my father was surprisingly free. In his amiable way, Hugh asked,

"Sir, do you have a minute to talk?"

"Call me Charlie. What's your name, son?"

He reached out and shook my father's hand.

"Mr. Charlie, my name is Hugh Hicks."

"What can I do for you, Hugh?"

"Well, Mr. Charlie, I would like to know if you could use a bootblack in your shop. You see, I just moved here from New York, and I need work. I will, of course, pay you rent."

"Hmm, let me see. I have the space. How big is your shoe shine stand?"

"I don't have a stand yet, but I can make it small."

My father smiled at him, asking,

"Are you starting a new business?" "Yes, Mr. Charlie."

"Is this your first business, Hugh?" "Yes, Mr. Charlie."

"You sound more like a school teacher than a shoe shine boy. Why bootblack?"

"Mr. Charlie, I'm embarrassed to say that I am a college graduate who can't get a job anywhere."

After maybe a twenty-second pause, which I'm sure was an eternity to Hugh Hicks, my father replied,

"Okay, Hugh, let's give it a shot. I'll take a chance with you. We're closed tomorrow and Monday and reopen on Tuesday. I'll give you a key to the shop, and you can build your shoe stand over the weekend."

"God bless you, Mr. Charlie, I won't let you down!"

"Hugh, it won't be without cost to you. Your rent will keep the shop clean, and the shoe stand is to be made for only one chair. And by the way, my name is Charlie, not Mr. Charlie."

My first glimpse of Hugh Hicks was on that unusually slow Saturday. While working on the Hebrew sign, I noticed a Black man talking to my father in the front of the shop. I couldn't make out what they were saying, but by the smile on the man's face, I knew it was something good. The shop was closed on Sundays and Mondays, and when I arrived there with my father the following Tuesday, there was a double surprise. First, the shop was already open. Second, in the back of the shop was the same Black fellow building a shoe shine station. My father must have seen something special in this person to entrust him with the key to the place. Soon after his coming aboard, my father put a sign in the window: "Bootblack on premises."

Hugh Hicks was a graduate of the City College of New York. He proved to be a great friend to me, and my father enjoyed his company. A humble man, he had a good heart and never had an unkind thought in his head. He made his way north from a poor area in Alabama, hopeful of furthering his education. He told me that after he graduated high school with high marks, he worked at random menial jobs to earn enough money to get to New York.

He was twenty-two when he finally entered City College, four years older than his graduating class. He earned a degree in Business Administration but couldn't find work. Hugh understood why some potential employers required him to show them his college diploma in the interview, but that didn't discourage him. However, when they got back to him, he was inevitably told that someone else got the job. While searching for work in areas suited to his education, he had little choice, so he took a variety of part-time jobs. He worked in a supermarket as both a checkout and stock clerk, as well as as an assistant in a local library. While working in a construction company, he learned carpentry skills. His last project before he was let go was helping to create an elaborate three-seat bootblack stand. He had an active role in its construction and was proud of his work.

I spent a great deal of time with Huge Hicks. I learned several lasting things from him. Up to then, there were very few Black people in my life — only Horace, the Crawfords, and my good friend Clarence Williams and his family. One of the things that I learned from knowing Hugh Hicks was that my father did not have a prejudiced bone in his body. In fact, a number of years earlier, some bigots tried to stop customers from coming into one of his barber shops because he cut the hair of Black men. This so enraged him that he punched one of the protesters in the jaw and knocked him out. Dad was arrested and cautioned but never regretted his action. Charlie Beans sized Hugh up and took him under his wing as he would have any sincere, hard-working self-starter down on his luck.

ON THE MOVE

CHAPTER 7

OUR WORLD FALLS APART

Everything was going well for us. I had close friendships with Horace and Grace. My father's business was a success. Hugh was making a decent living. My mother and sisters, and I felt secure in our new life. In March 1957, after a routine visit to one of her doctors, my mother was tested and soon learned she had breast cancer. Wasting no time, my father had her transferred from a hospital in Monticello to New York City's New York Presbyterian Hospital, where she had to undergo immediate surgery. A double mastectomy. While still in the hospital, she was also diagnosed with lung cancer and began treatment. On our last visit, she was sitting up peacefully in bed under a frightening-looking oxygen tent. We were only permitted to speak to her through the tent. We were not allowed to open the tent to kiss her goodbye, but when it was time to leave, each of us threw her a kiss. As I started to follow my father and sisters out of the room, my heart nearly stopped when my mother called out,

"Frankie, come back." When I approached her bedside, she pulled the tent curtain aside and told me to kiss her. I didn't know it then, but we were kissing goodbye forever.

Mom and Dad.

One dark, early morning in April, we were all awakened by the insistent ringing of the telephone. I was frightened by the sound of my father's agonized voice, pleading with the person on the other end of the phone,

"No, no! It's not true! Please don't tell me this. It's not true!" My mother had died.

I was thirteen when my sisters and I entered Lucia's funeral parlor on the 184th Street. The dreadful image of my mother lying in an open casket stayed with me for over twenty years before I was able to picture her as she lived. I'm sure that disturbing sight contributed to my sister Barbara's eventual nervous breakdown.

Once again, the Lucido family had come to a fork in the crooked road of our lives. Returning to Ferndale, my father made arrangements to sell the barbershop and move back to The Bronx. He made provisions in the contract of sale, stipulating that Hugh's bootblack business was to remain rent-free until the new owner finished paying off his financial obligation to my father or Hugh decided to leave. I always regretted having to part ways with Hugh at that time. He always saw the best in people and, in many ways, was like an older brother to me. About eighteen months later, when my father received the final payment, he told me that Hugh was still in the shop and that he'd also purchased a financial interest in the bowling alley. When I questioned him about Hugh, he said to me,

"He's doing okay. Never worry about Hugh Hicks. The man has a head on his shoulders. He's well-liked in Liberty and safe from the bullshit crap he came from."

Until Dad was able to get back on his feet, he arranged for Barbara and me to live temporarily with my mother's siblings while Vita stayed briefly in an orphanage. I was placed with my Aunt Josephine and Uncle Frank in an overcrowded two-bedroom apartment on Grote Street, just south of 183rd Street. I lived there with my aunt and uncle and five cousins — Pasquale (Pat), Vera, Natalie, Marie and Gloria. I shared a bed with my cousin Pat. Barbara stayed with our Uncle Tony and Aunt Edith and their young daughter, Abigail, on Arthur Avenue.

Lessons In Finance

Before we could all live together again, my father assured my sisters and me that he would be working hard to reunite us in an apartment of our own again. He also explained to me that he had left with Uncle Frank an allowance of fifty cents a day for me. I was to ask my uncle for it each day. I learned my first lesson in finance from Uncle Frank. At the end of the first day, I had spent thirty cents on treats for my cousins and me. The following morning, I asked my uncle for my fifty cents. He asked me how much I spent. I pulled two dimes from my pants pocket and said,

"Thirty cents." He then took thirty cents from a jar and told me,

"There you go. You now have fifty cents."

Something was wrong here. By day three, with twenty-five cents in my back pocket, when asked how much I spent, I held out my empty hand and told him,

"Fifty cents."

"My God, you spent all that money?"

"Yeah. There are a lot of kids in this house, and we all like ice cream."

After the fourth day of spending "all" my allowance, he never again asked me what I spent. The day we moved into our new apartment, I handed my father about a dollar fifty in change. He asked me why I had this much change left over.

"If I tell you you, will you promise not to say anything to Uncle Frank?"

"Of course."

When I told him what my uncle had been doing, he laughed out loud and told me how proud he was of me for beating the man at his own game. Dad refused to take the leftover money.

That summer, I got a job at Arthur Avenue Market. Former three-term mayor Fiorello Laguardia created ten retail food markets throughout the city's immigrant neighborhoods. The Arthur Avenue Market housed over one hundred vendors. The large majority were Italian- immigrants, selling meats, fish, vegetables, cold cuts, imported cheeses, nuts, olive oil, and canned goods. My job was to sell fruits and vegetables from a stand just opposite the now-famous Mike's Deli.

Drawing i made when I was 14 years old

My employer was a forceful, pushy, and loud, rotund Italian woman named Lina. I was to re-stock the bins, weigh and sell the produce, and above all, make sure the customers kept their hands off the fruit! Customers had to point out the particular pieces of fruit they wanted to buy, and I would place them in a brown paper bag. I soon found out that she had the market's best fruits and vegetables, and I never saw anyone dare to feel Lina's fruits! On my first day of work, Lina insisted I arrive two hours early to show me the ropes. So at 6 am, well before the crowds arrived, she placed on the counter a medium-sized brown paper bag with several apples in it. She told me to look inside the bag to tell her what I saw. In broken English, she said,

"Looka, inna da baga, whata you see?" "Apples, Lina."

"Okay, leta me see you weigha da apples."

Hanging from crudely made wood brackets was a farm scale. It had a large clock-like white face attached to a round porcelain-coated metal basket.

"One and a half pounds."

"Atsa vedy good. Howa mucha you chaga?"

"At twenty cents a pound, thirty cents. Am I right?"

"*Molto bene, bouno*, atas good. Takea off, anda givame tha baga." Holding the bag in her hand, she said, "Now you watcha me."

She placed the bag into the basket. Magically, the scale showed two pounds, and the cost went up to forty cents. I had just learned the fine art of "thumbing" the scale.

By the end of that summer, my father found work and was able to sub-let an apartment from a neighborhood friend for two months where we could all live before moving into an apartment of our own on Crotona Avenue near 187th Street.

CHAPTER 8

A DARK TIME FOR US

Back in our old neighborhood, I reconnected with some of my old friends from the early days and made new ones, but it was still a dark time for us. My mother's siblings had deserted us. Aunt Josie and Uncle Tony had risen to the occasion by taking Barbara and me in when we were in desperate need in the aftermath of my mother's death. And then they disappeared.

With my mother gone, my sisters and I were left mostly on our own. Vita was more of a mother to Barbara and me than Charlie Beans, who was a father to the three of us. We hardly ever saw him at the dinner table that Vita always set. She cooked our meals, cleaned our clothing, and made sure holidays like Christmas and Easter were observed.

Barbara, who had been the closest of all of us to our mother, had a nervous breakdown at age fourteen. I have no memory of Charlie Beans' role in Barbara's sad story other than his admitting my young sister to Jacobi Hospital after a diagnosis of schizophrenia. She was soon transferred to Harlem Valley State Hospital in Wingdale, New York. Wrapped up in himself, he never once went to see her at any of the mental institutions where she lived out her days. I spent several years making monthly visits to her until she was transferred to an assisted living facility for the mentally ill on Long Island that was paid for by my mother's Social Security. I continued to visit her periodically over the years. We were always pleased to see each other, and I was happy to know that she had friends, though these were always somber occasions for me.

I've always been convinced that if my aunts and uncle had been there to help us, my younger sister would not have been institutionalized for the rest of her life.

CHAPTER 9

THE DONISIS

My mother's family history was a tough one. The extended Donisi family was always poor. My mother's mother, Elvira Donisi, died in 1922 at age thirty-six as the result of an infection after an abortion. My maternal grandfather, Achille Donisi, was a cobbler by trade. In 1925, he abandoned my mother and her three siblings, placing them in an orphanage, and went back to Italy. He returned in 1937 with a new wife who was twenty-nine years younger than their father. When we first met this new step-grandmother, she'd been widowed since 1951 and was living with five daughters in a one-bedroom apartment on the second floor of 560 East 189th Street. My mother and her siblings did not welcome these newcomers.

There were many tensions within the family. Anna and Josie eventually became estranged from their younger brother, Tony, because he married a Jewish woman. His wife was our Aunt Edith, whom my sisters and I loved dearly. My aunts treated her condescendingly, often mimicking her accent, which always made me uncomfortable. An easygoing, quiet man, my Uncle chose to distance himself from the family entirely to avoid the insulting way Anna and Josie behaved toward his wife. Those two aunts also seemed to harbor a dislike of my father for reasons I could never understand. Were they jealous of his success? Did they disapprove of his running around? I never heard him speak ill of them. While my mother was alive, neither of them had any problem arriving on our doorstep with their families unannounced, just in time for Sunday dinners. My father always received them cordially.

As for Grandma Italia, we loved her as much as we could have loved the real grandmothers we never knew. According to her daughter, Anne, she kept a tight leash on her children. They were to stay on the stoop and play only on their own, or else! These step-aunts were more like sisters to us than aunts. If you were to ask any of

My half-aunts Alba, Vicki, Dora, Anne

these young girls, living on 189th Street with their loving mother was very good. The girls ranged in age from Dora, twenty years old, to Marie, who was eight.

The three closest to my age were Alba, Anne, and Victoria (Vicki), ages eighteen, fifteen, and sixteen. I spent a lot of time playing with Anne and Vicki after school and on weekends. They lived across the street from PS 45, where we all went to school together. Their mother's kind and affectionate presence was a great comfort to my sisters and me after our mother died. When we were older, my friends and I would often run into Anne at one of The Bronx nightclubs. We would always look out for her, though she could handle herself very easily without any help from us. There was no mincing of words with Anne. She called it as she saw it. She was always a lady, but you wouldn't want to cross her! Vicki's temperament was more reflective and analytical. She took the time to think things through and convincingly argued her points. She spoke; we listened!

Vita's Story

My step-aunts, their mother, and I, all supported Vita when she came out as a lesbian at age twenty-two. I can't say whether I'd ever thought about her sexual orientation before then. She was my big sister, five years older and six years ahead of me in school. It was almost as if we lived in two different worlds. In Ferndale, I was the boy in the family, doing my own thing and enjoying hanging out in my father's barbershop while she and Barbara helped my mother around the house.

Vita was a good-looking girl, fun to be with, who easily made friends wherever we lived. My mother picked on Vita a lot. I always thought it was because she was the oldest.

Some years later, after her coming out and before she moved to the West Coast, Vita confided in me. She told me our mother abused her verbally and emotionally because of her sexual identity. Mom nagged her about her appearance and generally found fault with her. Vita constantly felt her disapproval. I was appalled to hear how our mother treated my sister. A painful memory was immediately awakened as I recalled an incident from our childhood in Ferndale. One evening, when my father was absent, the three of us were sitting at the kitchen table while Mom was serving us dinner. My sisters and I were acting silly, laughing uncontrollably, and having fun. I was the instigator. Suddenly, my mother shouted at Vita;

"This is a dinner table, not a playground. Stop acting like an animal and eat your dinner!"

We lowered our voices, but now we were all giggling hysterically when my mother again scolded only Vita,

"If you don't stop it, you'll eat like a dog under the sink!"

Thinking that Barbara or I were next to be chastised, I continued to horse around until my mother picked up Vita's plate from the table, placed it under the kitchen sink, and yelled out to her!

"You want to act like a dog; eat your dinner as a dog!"

It shocked and disgusted me. A flood of sadness came over me at the sight of my sister sitting under the sink with a fork in her hand.

Before she moved to the West Coast, Vita got a job with The New York Telephone Company and moved to an apartment of her own off Pelham Parkway. Through Dora, she befriended someone who lived in the same building as our step-aunts. This woman, Arlene, became her significant other, and when she relocated to California, Vita soon followed. Once there, she worked for the Copley Press newspaper chain. She and Arlene lived together.

Several years later, Arlene committed suicide. Distraught, Vita needed to change her life, so she moved to Eugene, Oregon. In California, she had joined the Sons of Italy. This fraternal organization of Italian Americans started in 1905, always had many women participants. In Oregon, Vita became an active and valued member, helping to organize a newly formed chapter. In 2017, the organization changed its name to The Sons and Daughters of Italy. This association with her roots offered her some solace. She made many friends in Eugene and lived there for many years, her cheerful disposition intact.

When she let me know she was terminally ill, I spoke to her doctor, who advised me that she only had a short time to live. I flew right to Oregon to spend the few remaining days with her. Her last wish was to be cremated and have her ashes scattered in Ferndale's Mongaup River, which, of course, I honored.

MY FATHER'S UNIVERSE

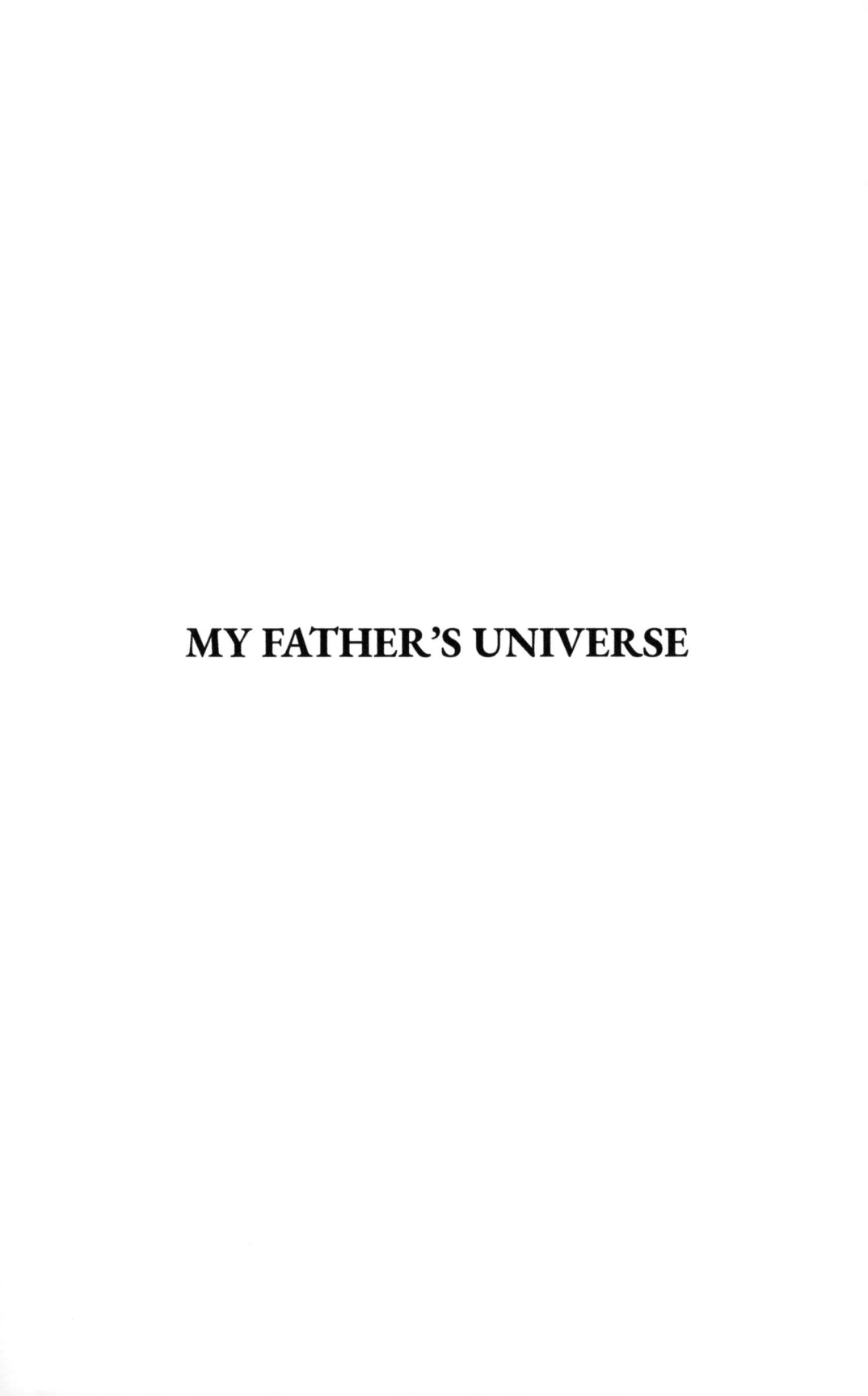

CHAPTER 10

THE SHACK

Just south of 187th Street, on Crotona Avenue, directly across the street from our apartment, was a sizable patch of land. An oversized shed that once housed small gardening equipment was now a decrepit clubhouse on a corner of the property. Its dull green walls were discolored by years of cigarette smoke. The only lighting in the place came from two flickering fluorescent bulbs. Squeezed into a corner was a small closet with a pull-chain toilet and a sink marred by rust stains.

J&B Scotch, a jug of homemade wine, a bottle of anisette, and a hot plate used for making espresso sat on a chipped porcelain table that served as the makeshift bar. A small open cabinet, with bar glasses and half a dozen espresso cups, hung above it. The paint-blistered back door led outside to a bocce alley and a carefully tended garden planted with tomatoes, cabbage, and grape vines. Straight out of central casting, a wrinkled-faced old-timer from Sicily owned the property. His shack was known as The Club to locals who would stop in after work for drinks and espresso sweetened with anisette — and for loud, bantering Italian card games, such as Briscola and Scopa. They also played Morra, a very popular and vociferous hand game that dates back to ancient Greece and Rome.

My father soon became a fixture at the club and started dropping in almost daily. It wasn't long before he was up to his old tricks, gambling, partying with his friends, and looking for money-making schemes. He was very well known in the neighborhood and shrewdly started bringing pals and acquaintances into the tiny shack. With his outgoing personality and ability to speak Italian dialects from Naples, Sicily, and Calabria, he soon became the unofficial manager. The old man, who took a liking to him, complained that he did not like the increasing number of new people in his club. As Charlie Beans had calculated, the owner eventually asked him if he would like to buy the property, quoting a price of $30,000. A crafty negotiator, Beans told him he didn't have that kind of money, especially since the shack would have to be demolished, and what would he do with a vacant lot?

Several months later, the old man, tired from all the new activity, again approached my father. He agreed to a $5,000 down payment, in cash, to be followed by a total of $15,000 in regular installments over the next five years. With financing from a bank, plus a little extra help from his "connections," he purchased the property and constructed a substantial building, setting aside outdoor spaces for parking and two bocce alleys.

Compliments of Maurice, of Sam's Resturant in Dobbs Ferry NY.

He had no trouble selling his barber shop, and in late 1959, he held a grand opening of his new venture. It was soon a popular hangout, well-established in the neighborhood. From Monday to Friday, from 11 am to 4 pm, ten to twenty regulars would be in the place. These were blue-collar workers and local businessmen on lunch breaks or retirees stopping in for a game of bocce or a cup of espresso and the neighborhood gossip. After 6 pm, many of the same guys would return, joining the evening crowd. The weekend poker game started on Friday evenings and, at times, would not finish until the next day, just before the Saturday morning customers began to gather. Many a game would span all three days of the weekend. With the cops turning a blind eye to his gambling operation, the club became such a success that Dad owned it free and clear within two years.

Sundays were special. They had a fun, festive vibe. Men from all walks of life would meet and mingle. Doctors and lawyers, business owners and construction workers, and the occasional mix of Mafia types and police could all turn up at the same time. Tables filled with card players and conversationalists enjoying drinks, sandwiches, espresso, and Italian pastries. The bocce alleys overflowed with players and spectators.

A Timely Tip

The poker game was a serious activity. Five percent of each pot was cut for the house. Other than Charlie Beans, only three people were allowed to cut the game. Two men who came from my father's hometown in Sicily — Cousin Frank, a tailor by trade, and Joe Fats, a civil engineer — and one sixteen-year-old boy, me.

When I was not in school, Dad let me arrange my shifts at the club around my days and nights out with my friends. On average, I worked there once each weekend. I served drinks and snacks in addition to cutting the poker game. When not working in the club, I continued to be employed by Eddie the Carpenter as his helper. Custom-made professional poker chips were used at the club: five-dollar blue and one-dollar green, imprinted with "CB," for Charlie Beans. Sitting on a high billiard chair, at the close of each game, I would tally the chips and call out the amount of the pot, sliding the house's five-percent take to the side for the winner to count. Once the total was confirmed, I'd remove the house's share and drop it into a locked box. Because I was so young, once they got to know me, all I had to do was call out the number and hold the five percent in my hand, and no one questioned it.

One night, as usual, Joe Fats left his chips on the table and got up to stretch his legs and take a break. This time, he specifically asked me to join him, using my Italian nickname,

"Ciccio, take a break. This is going to be a long night. Have an espresso with me."

Out of respect, I didn't hesitate. I asked Cousin Frank to sit in for me for a few minutes. In his slightly accented English, speaking slowly, Joe quietly reprimanded me,

"Your father is a man of respect. You will disgrace his name if anyone learns what you are doing."

"What did I do?"

"You know what you were doing, I'm warning you, if I see you clipping chips again, I will tell your father."

Embarrassed and to conceal my larceny, I replied,

"Joe, I thought I was doing something good for my father, but the way you explain it…I'm so sorry."

"I know, Ciccio. You have a lot to learn."

CHAPTER 11

IN THE DRIVER'S SEAT

Things were really going well for me and for the two most influential figures in my life, Charlie Beans and Eddie the Carpenter. I was happy my dad was doing all the things he loved: playing cards, socializing, drinking, eating well, and making plenty of money — all at the same time, every day! I was making more money than I ever had, both in the club and working with Eddie. Eddie himself was about to start an unexpected new chapter in his life.

One Sunday in 1963, he dropped by the club with Claire Goodman, an attractive divorced mother with two young children. Claire lived in his sister's building, and soon after they met, they became an item. They had come to share with us the good news that they had just become engaged to be married. Then and there, Eddie asked me to be his best man. I was honored! My father shouted out his congratulations, "Drinks all around!" In June of that year, Eddie and Claire were married by a rabbi in a kosher restaurant near the Grand Concourse. It was a joyous occasion, with their families and close friends in attendance. I was almost as happy as Eddie because I knew he would never be lonely again.

"The Drop"
(I've Never Seen This in the Movies)

One Saturday afternoon, Dad had me drive him to a club at 181st Street and Broadway in upper Manhattan. I was happy to drive him anywhere in his brand-new car, an Oldsmobile Starfire convertible. That day, I learned about "The Drop." I double-parked the car while he went into a loft building on Broadway. When he got back, he told me to drive twenty blocks south. I asked him what we were doing. He said we were going to a few Goulash joints to make a "Drop." Goulash joints were clubs about the same size as ours but run by Jewish owners. It was an unwritten rule among non-mob club owners to support other clubs that were also partially under the influence of the Mafia. My father told me that Jewish mobsters controlled the clubs we were visiting that day. It soon became clear to me these drops were really a great excuse for Dad to get to lower Manhattan to have a meal at a favorite Sicilian restaurant on Tenth Street, where he would invariably meet friends from the old country.

Trooper

As a nineteen-year-old, I often had my father's expensive car available, the deep red "Garnet Mist" convertible. Driving around the neighborhood, that car was a status symbol for me among my friends. Late one Saturday afternoon in July, I was driving north on the Connecticut Turnpike, I-95, with Mike N and two other friends. We had met some girls in a nightclub a week earlier, and they'd invited us to a party they were having. Top-down, radio blaring, and speeding at seventy-five miles an hour, we were on our way to Stratford, Connecticut. Not a care in the world until a Connecticut State trooper came up behind me with his lights swirling.

"What's your hurry? Do you know you were speeding? License and registration!"

I said nothing and did as he asked.

"You're from The Bronx. What are you doing in Connecticut?"

"We're going to a party in Stratford, Officer. I didn't realize we were speeding; I'm really sorry." Looking at me suspiciously, he said, "This is an expensive car," then asked, "Who is Charles Lucido?" I explained this was my father's car and that if I got a summons, it would be the last time I'd be allowed to drive it. I was trying anything not to get ticketed.

"Crotona Avenue? Isn't that in the Little Italy section of The Bronx?" Hearing this from him, I figured out two things. He immediately noticed that I lived in Little Italy, and we were forty-five miles away from home. Knowing some police were "on the pad" in my neighborhood, I put two and two together. I figured that seeing four Italian teenagers in an expensive car owned by an Italian might make this guy open to a payoff.

"Yes, Officer, that's where I'm from. My father is working in his club today, and let me take the car."

"Where is your father's club?"

"It's on Crotona Avenue, across the street from where I live."

"Listen carefully to me. I'm letting you go for now, but if I find you going even one mile over the limit on your way back, I will pull you in. Is that clear?"

"You've got my word, Officer. I will stay below the limit. Thank you so much." I was proud of myself, thinking how smart I was for talking my way out of a summons. Especially when the guys with me in the car, who'd kept very quiet, congratulated me for my fast thinking.

About a month later, before going out to try and hustle a pool game, Mike and I were having dinner with my father in the club. It was a weekday, and the place was quiet. Cousin Frank was the manager that night and had made Dad's favorite lentil soup. He placed a steaming bowl in front of each of us, and we began to sip the delicious soup in silence. After a few minutes, without raising his eyes, my father asked us a question,

"What were you doing on the Connecticut Throughway?" Mike and I glanced at each other, surprised.

"Throughway? What throughway?"

After a quick pause from sipping his soup, still facing down at his plate, he went on, "Cut the bullshit. You *chooches* cost me fifty bucks."

Tombstone

I put a lot of miles on that car, driving with friends to Orchard Beach in The Bronx and as far away as Jones Beach on Long Island. One day, on the way home from Jones Beach, I noticed an exit to St. Raymond's Cemetery, where my brother Carlo and mother shared the same gravesite. Five years had passed since my mother's death, and I had never visited her grave. That night, alone in our big apartment, the grim memory of the scene that confronted my sisters and me in 1957 flashed across my mind. It was the image of my beautiful mother lying in an open casket at Lucia's Funeral Home — a vision that continued to haunt me for many years. On my first day off work that week, I drove to the cemetery with a small bouquet of flowers next to me on the passenger seat. The gravesite was conveniently located on a side road in the old section of St. Raymond's. I slowly drove down the road until I reached my mother's grave. Suddenly, I felt agitated to see that her name was not carved into the headstone.

Standing alone, my brother's and mother's remains resting beneath the ground in front of me, my heart was heavy. I was overwhelmed with sadness and regret and long-suppressed feelings of deprivation and loss. Then another emotion took hold — anger at my father, who had not had the decency to follow through to mark my mother's final resting place.

Before leaving, I closed my eyes and brought to mind some of the happiest times I had with Carlo and my Mom. I carefully placed the flowers at the grave and left the cemetery. I located a monument place nearby and ordered my mother's inscription added to the headstone.

That evening, my father was surprised to see me at the club because it was my night off. He was at the poker table when I came in, and I asked him to give me a minute to talk. He had Cousin Frank take his seat, and we walked over to the end of the bar. Not wasting any time, I said,

"Dad, today I went to the cemetery for the first time since Mom's death. Did you ever make a visit?"

"No, Frankie, I didn't. I should make a visit."

"I can't believe you! You didn't even have the decency to put your wife's name on the headstone!"

Without waiting for his excuses, I walked out. He followed me onto the street. "Frankie, I'm so sorry. I'm just a selfish, self-centered man, always thinking only about myself. I will go tomorrow first thing."

"Don't bother. After all these years, I'm doing your job. I'm having it done." Taking out a roll of bills from his pocket and peeling off three or four $100s, he said,

"Here, Frankie. I'm paying for it."

"Keep your money. It's done. I've taken care of it."

Without looking back, I hurried across the street, where Mike was waiting for me in his car, and we drove off.

CHAPTER 12

THE UGLIEST DAY IN MY LIFE

It was an early morning in July 1963, one month before my twentieth birthday. The uniquely sweet scent of freshly washed streets filled the air as only a New Yorker can appreciate. The warm sun hitting my face as I crossed Crotona Avenue to the club filled me with happiness. In my arms, I held a restaurant-size, shiny, stainless steel coffee urn containing freshly made espresso for the club.

My father was sitting at a table, having coffee and a buttered roll. He was well-tanned, cheerful, and looked youthful in his white short-sleeve shirt and tan shorts. I placed the thermos on the bar and started cleaning up from the night before. He finished his breakfast and was adjusting the tables and chairs. While he brushed the green felt on the poker table, someone knocked firmly on the club's front door. Alone with my father, I looked through the peephole, observing two men standing there. I told my father that two well-dressed men were outside and that they looked like detectives.

"No problem, let them in."

I opened the door. The bigger man, over six feet tall, made way for the slightly built man who had no expression on his face. Following the smaller man, who was about the same height as my father, the big guy smiled and thanked me. Charlie Beans recognized them and cheerfully welcomed them in. As I closed and locked the door, I was horrified by what I heard coming from the smaller man's mouth.

"You fucking cocksucker, you no good piece of shit. Who the fuck do you think you are?"

My father, shocked, meekly responded,

"Mickey, what did I do?

"You fucking scumbag, are you telling me you don't know what the fuck you did?" Dad was silent.

"Answer me, you fucking shit!"

"Mickey, with all due respect, I don't know what I did, and I'm so sorry for offending you."

"You have the fucking balls to run this fucking joint without my permission? I should have your legs broken, you cocksucker! Starting this Monday and every Monday, you prick, I want you to come to my place each week with $500. Do you understand me, you fucking shit?"

In undeniable defeat, my father replied,

"I do, Mickey."

Mickey turned and started for the door. He glanced at me, icy and inhuman. I could have spit in his face. The big man unlocked and opened the door. As he exited, following Mickey, he turned his head towards my father and gave a sympathetic shrug of his shoulder.

Modeste Barra, known as "Mickey Morris," was a soldier in the Genovese crime family. The big man with him was Aldo Bright Eyes Serra, a button man, a Mafia soldier in Mickey's crew. Both men had known my father for over twenty-five years, from when they all lived in Italian East Harlem. The thought never entered Charlie Beans' mind that he had to get permission to operate the club. My father was familiar with Mafia rules about territorial control of gambling and other illegal activities. But he naively thought his twenty-five-year friendship with Mickey, dating back to their youth, excused him from the usual protocols. Dazed and bewildered, he put me in charge and left the club. I didn't know that he set out immediately for Bensonhurst, Brooklyn. I wasn't aware that some of Dad's Brooklyn cousins held the same rank as Mickey and were with the Gambino Mafia family. He couldn't ask for help from any of the neighborhood guys since everyone deferred to Mickey, so he went to his cousins for advice.

As the day progressed, the club was packed as usual; every table was occupied, and a few men were waiting to play poker. There was a line for the bocce courts, and everyone was enjoying their drinks. Cousin Frank and I were running things. My father returned around 3 pm. Without a word spoken, he forced a smile, pinched my cheek, and went on to the poker table. He took out the chips, sat down, and, in his usual upbeat manner, bellowed out,

"Okay, who wants to play poker?"

Nothing more was said, and I left well enough alone, hopeful that this would soon become a forgotten event we could put behind us. I had no doubt how deeply humiliated my father felt, having been so savagely belittled in front of his son on that terrible day.

CHAPTER 13

PAYMENT IN FULL

The following Friday, I was off work and had just gotten home from the cleaners, where I'd picked up the suit I was going to wear later that night. Our six-and-a-half-room apartment was now occupied only by my father and me. Some parts of the three bedrooms were also used to store cases of bootlegged liquor and other illicit luxury goods acquired for a song through contacts in the neighborhood. We used what we needed or wanted, and the rest was sold to people we knew. (A famous Rock and Roll teen idol once came to our apartment and bought a mink coat.)

I started searching for a pair of brown shoes but was having little luck as I rummaged through the three rooms used for storage. They were filled with racks of hanging suits, fur coats, cases of J&B Scotch, and boxes of electric shavers and other supplies. An hour must have passed before I remembered that I'd put the shoes away on an upper shelf of a closet. When I finally found the shoebox, it appeared closer to the edge of the shelf than where I had originally placed it. As I was taking it down, I noticed a brown paper grocery bag behind it that wasn't there when I put the shoes away. I had to stand on a chair to reach it. It felt bulky and heavy as I pulled it forward. I stepped off the chair and put the bag, tightly folded to conceal its contents, on the bed. Inside was a loaded black Beretta pistol.

My heart started beating so hard that l lost my breath. I sat down on the bed and began to cry. I was sure I knew its purpose. The bullets in this weapon were to be delivered to Morris, along with his first and final five hundred dollar payment! The next forty minutes are unreeled like scenes in a film noir. Regaining control of myself, careful not to touch the weapon, I took the bag with the gun to the car and placed it into the wheel-well, that held the spare tire. Entering the club, I found my father alone at the bar, having a bowl of lentil soup. I looked straight into his eyes with a stare as icy as the one I had received from Mickey Morris and told him,

"I found the gun you hid in the closet. I'm telling you now that you will either have no life or no son because if you, by any chance, get away with it, you will never see me again. I'm getting rid of it." He glared at me, but I didn't give him a chance to speak.

"I know exactly what you felt last week and how small Mickey made you feel. I know what you intend to do to save face. I know this because, most likely, I would want to do the same thing if it was my son who was present at such a horrible event. The difference is that I would realize that having my son is far more important to me than how someone made me look in his eyes. These people are not your friends, and there is nothing they can ever say or do that will lessen the man my father is to me." Without waiting for a response, I left the club and drove to the tip of Hunts Point, where I threw the paper bag and its contents into the murky water of the East River.

I didn't show up for work on Saturday. I called Joe Fats and asked him to do me a favor and keep an eye on my father because he wasn't feeling 100% and to keep my call to himself. After a night out, late on Sunday, I went to the club with my best friend, Mike. The poker game was on, my father was playing, and the guys were waiting for a seat at the table, as usual. When he saw us, Dad finished his hand and offered his seat to one of the waiting players. He looked at Mike and me and said,

"Let me buy you two bums a drink."

Nothing more was said. We had our drinks with him and left.

Monday night, at dinner in the club, Dad opened the conversation by saying, "Guess what? My cousin Pauly arranged a meeting with Morris and settled on two hundred bucks a week. He was pissed off at me because all I had to do was run my plans by Mickey in the first place and mention that Pauly was my cousin. Dad was embarrassed since it simply had not occurred to him, given his long relationship with Mickey. To lighten the conversation, I said jokingly,

"Jesus Christ, Dad, you, with all your wise guy friends, you didn't know this?

Dad, you're losing it."

"Frankie, I'm not like these guys, and that's why I get along with them."

"Dad, only a real shit of a man would have acted the way Mickey acted in front of the guy's son."

"Yes, you're right. Even Tony Blue Eyes stopped by late Sunday to apologize for his boss' outbursts. I'm over it, and I'm grateful and proud of the way you handled me. I love you."

Mickey Morris got his weekly take. He was happy. Strange as it may seem, he would occasionally stop by like any other neighborhood guy, smiling at me and my father as if nothing had ever happened. Sometimes, he'd drop a hundred-dollar bill on the bar and buy a round of drinks for all. Drinks at that time were about forty cents, and most of Mickey's gestures would actually cost no more than twenty bucks. The balance went to the house. From time to time, on my visits to the club, I'd notice men I didn't know would come into the club, drop a fifty or a hundred dollar bill on the bar, and buy a round of drinks for all.

CHAPTER 14

AN UNSANCTIONED HIT

I continued to work for Eddie, putting in much less time at the club while starting my move away from my father. I rented a place of my own on Astor Avenue, one block north of Pelham Parkway. Eventually, I decided it was time for me to show my face at least and see how my father was doing. One Saturday night, I stopped by the club with my friend Mike to say hello and have a drink. Things seemed normal, with the usual number of people drinking and playing cards. The poker table was running hot. One thing was different. Dad's appearance had changed drastically. He had lost at least fifteen pounds since the last time I'd seen him.

"Dad, are you okay? You don't look well at all."

"I'm fine, Frankie, just getting older and eating less."

Mike and I enjoyed our drinks with him, then left for our night out.

A few weeks later, at a nightclub near my apartment, one of my friends mentioned that Tony Blue Eyes was found dead up in Westchester. We were all surprised, especially me, because I had often seen him at my father's club. Not long after, I wanted to check in on my father again. When I arrived at the club, I was shocked to see the fence padlocked and the club closed. I rushed across the street to Dad's building and went up to see him. When I opened the door to his apartment, I discovered Charlie Beans sitting with Joe Fats, watching TV. He had a glass of his usual J&B in hand. Joe Fats looked comfortable with a glass of wine and a plate of cheese in front of him.

"What happened, Dad? Why is the club closed? Are you sick? You look very thin."

"I'm okay. Frankie, I'm not sick."

I wasn't satisfied with that.

"Joe, you're our closest friend. Now tell me what's wrong with my father!"

"Ciccio, his health is fine. The club was closed by the police."

My father and Joe proceeded to tell me what had occurred weeks earlier, shortly before Mike and I visited Dad at the club.

Mickey Morris' moving in on the club increased business greatly, but not without serious consequences. After that, the impression got around that it was "Mickey's Club." Many more Mafia guys have now become regulars. The fun-filled Sundays came to an end. With few exceptions, all of the upper-middle-class residents, who enjoyed the good fellowship of neighborhood friends, stopped coming. A year earlier, two of Mickey's underlings, Nicky R and Tony Blue Eyes, got into a fight that left one of them with a groin injury from a gunshot wound. Mickey put out an order throughout all the clubs and bars under his protection in The Bronx and Westchester. Those two wise guys must never be allowed in any of his places at the same time.

Joe Fats went on to describe what happened on the particular poker weekend that caused the club to close. Tony Blue Eyes was at the poker table. Cousin Frank was serving drinks and watching the door. No one came in on those poker nights without being identified through the peephole. Dad was playing at the table, too. There was a rap on the door. Cousin Frank looked through the peephole and, recognizing a familiar face, inadvertently let in Tony's enemy. My father, seeing this man, immediately gave up his seat to someone waiting to play. Hastily, he walked over and whispered,

"Nicky, I have to ask you to leave."

Nicky walked calmly toward the poker table, replying,

"Charlie, you know I respect you. I'm not here to make trouble. I just wanted to say hello, have a drink, and maybe sit in for a pot or two. I'll have a glass of whiskey and leave."

"Do I have your word, Nicky?"

"You have my word, Charlie."

My father hurried to the bar. No sooner had he finished pouring Nicky's drink when three gunshots rang out. Nicky's target was Tony Blue Eyes, the man who had shot him in the groin. Tony was now lying back in his chair with two bullets in his chest, his brains splashed against the wall. Nicky pointed the gun at Cousin Frank and told him to open the door to let in his accomplice. He turned to my father and said,

"Charlie, I'm sorry it had to be your place. Now take hold of one of his legs." Quickly pointing his gun at my father and three of the bystanders, he ordered each of them to pick up a limb.

"You guys, take his body out to the car parked out front."

He instructed everyone else to stay where they were until Charlie and the others returned.

"You will all leave when and how I tell you to."

When my father came back with the other three men, Nicky told everyone to leave three at a time, at two or three-minute intervals. He apologized to my father again and told him to pick two or three men to stay and help him clean up. My father was stunned, but thinking clearly enough not to want to impose any further on his customers. Fortunately, Joe Fats, Cousin Frank, and Enzo, one of the players, volunteered to stay and help him. Later, it became known that Nicky and his accomplice dumped the body in a wooded area somewhere around Hawthorne, New York. A week or two after the killing, state troopers raided the club and took my father and about thirty customers in for questioning. Dad thought they must have been tipped off by some of the card players who were in the club at the time of the killing.

Nicky R. disappeared entirely. It was rumored that he did not have permission to kill Tony Blue Eyes and was himself most likely knocked off under orders from Mickey Morris. Dad's sudden dramatic weight loss was caused by his witnessing a cold-blooded murder just a few feet away from him, in the club, his second home.

I told my father I would continue to work at the club, now and then, until I finished school. Then I would be done. He said I could stop anytime I wanted.

SCHOOL DAZE

CHAPTER 15

PUBLIC SCHOOL AND ME

I was almost on the threshold of adulthood but was unformed in many ways. The days of helping out in my father's club were winding down, and I was working mostly part-time as a carpenter with Eddie. With a local diploma in hand, I'd finally graduated high school, thanks to an understanding principal who had a soft spot for luckless kids like me. I walked out of the Bathgate Avenue exit of Roosevelt High, having benefitted very little from the education offered me. From early childhood, my schooling consisted of a patchwork of **six** different schools attended when my family was constantly moving around. We had moved back and forth from The Bronx to as far away as York, Pennsylvania, and Liberty, New York — living in four different apartments and one house.

On my own most of the time, without much parental supervision, I used my brain to devise as many ways as possible to avoid sitting in class. I could barely read and write. Knowing I was going to do poorly when called upon in class or fail when tested, I concentrated my energies on doing everything I could to get out of homework. My disruptive antics often caused my teachers grief. By the time I reached PS 45, junior high, many of my behavioral problems had become ingrained coping mechanisms. I was left back in the fifth grade and again in the seventh grade, where I was assigned to the "basket weaving" class for the kids who couldn't keep up. In my neighborhood, there was an Italian-American slang word for it, *boshkette* (pronounced "baw- SHKETT"). In any language, it meant the class for dumb kids.

My unproductive behavior continued well into high school. It ranged from regularly cutting classes and arguing with teachers to bringing phony doctors' notes to get me out of school early. I even made a removable cast for my right hand to pretend I was injured and couldn't write. All of the above led to frequent visits to the principal's office. In short, I preferred spending the daylight hours with losers on the street or in Cheech's poolroom on Arthur Avenue to being in any schoolroom. Teachers had little patience with me, with a few notable exceptions. In ninth grade, I had the great good fortune of having Mrs. Schurch as my homeroom teacher, as well as for English and History. She didn't discourage me from drawing pictures on the blackboard before she entered her classroom. She'd playfully call out,

"Okay, da Vinci, clear the board."

She put me and two other kids in charge of making three-dimensional holiday displays for the walls outside her class. She also encouraged the boys in her homeroom to join the basketball team. Finally, there was something for me to work on in school that didn't involve reading books. Up until then, I didn't play any sports. Being on a basketball court was a far cry from the poolroom. I, along with Victor Scarlino and John Delvechio, joined the team. To my surprise, I was halfway decent at the game.

At the end of that semester, Mrs. Schurch asked the three of us to write something for the yearbook about our basketball experiences. Victor declined, so John and I took on the task. We started writing about the games we played, the wins and losses. Halfway through, I told John it was pretty boring. Our team wasn't that great, and I suggested we write a poem, showing the reader that the results were less important than that we participated and tried hard. John agreed, and we had fun working together. Mrs. Schurch approved. It soon became clear that this kind teacher had taken a liking to Victor and me, two of her most troubled students. Just before we graduated from PS 45, she invited us to her home in suburban Westchester County for a weekend. She had a son our age, and we had a wonderful time in the country. Thanks to her, the ninth grade was the happiest school year of my young life.

Victor Scarlino, Mrs. Schurch and me

In high school, on one of my numerous trips to the principal's office, I was noisily expressing my frustrations with the demeaning way two particular teachers consistently treated me when I was overheard by Mr. Naughton, the art teacher, who was standing nearby. He asked me if I had any hobbies or special activities I enjoyed. Nobody had ever asked me questions like that before. I told him I liked working as a carpenter's helper and drawing pictures. I'd always loved to draw. In elementary school, my pictures were often selected to decorate the walls of the classroom.

This chance encounter was pivotal for me. He arranged for me to attend his classes with the principal, along with the shop teachers. These two men, Mr. Naughton and Mr. Chesner, rescued me and salvaged my self-esteem. And I was now freed from the two mean-spirited teachers and doing some schoolwork I actually enjoyed. In art class, I learned how to paint in watercolor and oil. Mr. Naughton reminded me that I came from a rich artistic heritage and suggested that I draw drawings of my Little Italy neighborhood and the people in it. Painting from memory, I created watercolors of the New York Botanical Garden, my "backyard" growing up. Working in oil, I painted portraits of old men from my father's club, whose faces I could still picture clearly. These pictures, in both mediums, were prominently displayed in the halls of Roosevelt High School for a long time.

Assigned to the shop class, I took it upon myself to draw a three-dimensional plan of a bookcase with specs. I showed it to Mr. Chesner, who quickly acknowledged I knew what I was doing. After testing my carpentry skills and correcting the way I used the table saw, he gave me a special assignment to build a multi-purpose bookcase for the shop based on my original plan. He was so pleased with the result that he asked me to design and build an additional set of bookcases to fit into an alcove. I became his assistant and enjoyed my new role guiding other students. Other than a mild interest in History and Social Studies, my focus was on Art and Design. For the first time in my life, I was at the top of the class!

CHAPTER 16

AFTER-SCHOOL ACTIVITIES

At PS 45 and Roosevelt High School, when the bell rang at 3 pm, I was free to roam the streets with my friends. All the kids in our age group knew not to mess with Ralphy M. He wasn't very tall, but because of his muscularity and toughness, he was viewed by most as the boss of all our neighborhood crews. The neighborhood had groupings of streets, each with its crew. Crews were usually composed of three to seven kids. There was the Belmont Avenue crew, Arthur Avenue crew, Crotona Avenue crew, and about six more crews named after the streets where the boss, or most popular kid of that crew, lived. Crews were inspired by those of the Mafia adults who lived among us. Whenever there were neighborhood functions, like church feasts or Police Athletic League gatherings, if Ralphy was there, it was customary to show him respect.

Occasionally, Ralphy put the word out to meet in the public playground to discuss planning a gang fight to avenge some real or imagined slight. All these fights were against Italian-American groups from other areas in The Bronx, like Morris Park Avenue, Gun Hill Road, or Country Club Road. There were rules for how fights were conducted that all gangs observed — no knives, bats, or sticks, just bare fists. The fight would be over when a gang leader called it quits or his guys gave up. Each gang's leader would pick two or three kids from one of his crews. Fortunately for the six or seven in our Crotona Avenue crew, we were not considered high in the toughness department.

"Ralphy, I'll Hold the Coats!"

One very cold winter day in 1961, the call went out to meet in the playground. The gang from Gun Hill Road had about seven guys waiting to fight to settle an incident in a bar over a girl. To my crew, it was the stupidest reason to have a gang fight. No matter, Victor S, Mikey R, Mike N, and I showed up. There must have been thirty guys from Ralphy's crews. The

Gun Hill Road boss chose three kids to fight. Now it was Ralphy's turn to pick three of our guys to fight. Sometimes, he would include himself.

My friends and I, the Crotona Avenue crew, were huddled close behind the Arthur Avenue bunch. Victor towered over all of us. We had never before been called to fight, but maybe because of the cold, Ralphy made a hasty decision this time. He pointed to Victor, Mike N, and me. Moving toward the circle where we were to fight, a frightened Mike whispered to an equally frightened me,

"Oh shit, we're finished!" Standing there in the frigid air, surrounded by about half a dozen shivering crews, we began to remove our coats. Suddenly, I heard my voice calling out loud enough for everyone to hear,

"Ralphy, I'll hold the coats!"

To my surprise, the entire crowd burst into laughter. The Gun Hill Road chief, who was laughing along with Ralphy, asked him,

"After this, do you really want to fight?"

Ralphy, shaking his head, answered,

"No way!"

Father George

PS 45 was located at 189th Street between Lorillard Place and Hoffman Street. Across the street from the school was Vita's Luncheonette (no relation to my sister), where most of my good school friends liked to meet for lunch. A buxom, no-nonsense woman in her forties, Vita was quick to protect anyone being pushed around by ruffians trying to break into the waiting line. Anyone who lived in the Little Italy neighborhood and went to Vita's knew of her famous open-faced mashed potato sandwich, a favorite of our kids. She would slice mini loaves of homemade Italian bread horizontally, scoop them out, and toast your half before filling it with her steaming mashed potatoes. Not knowing her mystery ingredients, I did learn years later that it was a mashed potato and scrambled eggs sandwich. The eggs were invisible.

Unfortunately, the character of my new friends was potentially toxic. I started hanging out with the roughest group of kids in my grade, mainly because they lived in my section of the neighborhood. Most of their pranks were considered petty, such as stealing a piece of fruit from a street vendor or shooting paper clips with rubber bands to break light bulbs in the hallways and vestibules of apartment buildings. Late one evening, Ralphy invited three of us for beers at his apartment when his family was out. After a few, he told us we were going to the Greek Orthodox Church on 183rd Street to get some money from the poor boxes. I couldn't believe what I was hearing. Afraid of being singled out as a coward, I said nothing and dutifully followed along with the others.

The street lights were shining through the beautiful stained glass windows, illuminating the small rectory. Wood-paneled walls, two ornate oak benches, and a brightly lit lamp on an end table completed the small room's furnishings. One guy said he was going into the church to check out the poor boxes. Ralphy and the rest of us sat on the benches. I'm asking myself, "What's next?" About two minutes passed, which felt like an hour to me when a priest entered the room. He was a tall, elegant-looking man, maybe in his late forties, just what you would envision a priest would look like. In a raspy, calm, almost inaudible voice, he introduced himself,

"Hello, boys. I'm Father George." Ralphy quickly got up and said,

"Hi, Father George. These are my friends," and walked right into Father George's office. The priest followed Ralphy and closed the door behind him. I asked the guys,

"What's going on? Why is Ralphy in there alone?"

"He's going to collect $3.00 from Father George," I was told.

"Why?"

"Father George is going to give Ralphy a blow job."

I was terrified and disgusted. I had a homosexual friend, and neither I nor any of my friends ever passed judgment on his sexuality. But a priest! I realized then that I was with the wrong group of guys. They made regular visits to the church, hoping to tap into the poor boxes and, at the same time, see Father George to make sure they didn't leave empty-handed. I thought to myself, "What kind of people are these that would take advantage of a situation like this?" My mind was racing! This can't be happening. If I leave, I'm a deserter, a punk, a weakling! I had to think fast. What could I do? All of a sudden, it came to me.

"Listen, let me go in next because it's getting late, and I better get home before my father."

No sooner had they agreed than Ralphy walked out of the room. I turned with a forced smile at Ralphy and walked past him into the office, closing the door behind me. Sitting on a straight-back chair was this so-called "man of the cloth." Before he could utter a word, I spoke,

"Father George, I can't do this. I want you to give me the $3.00, and I will walk out of here as if I did. No one will have to know."

"I understand, my son."

He reached under his cassock and pulled from his pocket three folded one-dollar bills. He handed me the money. I couldn't wait to get out of there. I moved close to the door and stood there, silently, waiting for some time to pass, when he asked,

"What's wrong, son? Are you not leaving?"

Without turning my head to look at him, I said,

"I'm leaving! Just wait a minute."

I left just enough time to give the impression that I went along with the program. Back in the rectory, I made sure my friends saw me counting the money. My heart was pounding, and I felt dirty. I stepped into the street and strolled along 183rd Street. When I turned onto Crotona Avenue, I threw the $3.00 into the sewer. I stopped hanging around with this bad group of guys. When seeing them around the neighborhood and questioned about where I'd been, luckily, I had a good and legitimate excuse. I had started working in my father's club.

An Old Friend Reappears

By the time I got to Roosevelt High, friction between the entrenched ethnic groups and the newer Black and Puerto Rican communities was increasing. There were three entrances to the school. We used Bathgate Avenue. Blacks and Puerto Ricans entered and exited on Washington Avenue. Fordham Road was the usual choice of the rest of the school population. In the Fifties and Sixties, there were two main Italian-American street gangs in our neighborhood, The Fordham Daggers and the infamous Fordham Baldies. The latter made up of older guys, had been around much longer and was feared throughout New York City. One day, a friend of mine, Frankie D, who was not in any gang but knew that Roosevelt High was considered Baldie turf, got into a verbal confrontation with two Black students who were wearing their gang jackets. Feeling territorial, Frankie told them to take them off, which they refused to do. He said nothing more to them but informed one of the Baldies.

The next day, the word went out. At 3 pm, when school let out, the Baldies were planning to beat up any Black kids they saw. They would be waiting for them at the Washington Avenue exit, which was the closest one to where those students lived.

By sheer coincidence, while walking up the steps leading to my next class, to my amazement, there was my old friend, Clarence Williams, walking down the same staircase towards me. We immediately stopped on the landing and embraced, and in the brief time we had, we recalled our former close friendship. I walked him to his class and made sure to tell him what the Baldies were going to do. I told him that if he had friends in the school, he and his friends would not have to leave the building from the Washington Avenue exit. Many innocent Black and Puerto Rican kids were injured that day, along with the two Black gang members. They were no match for the violent Baldies.

Not long after, Clarence and I met for burgers at a White Castle. I was pleased to learn he and three of his friends left school as I had instructed and were able to avoid the fight. The school year soon ended, and we each went on with our lives. We never saw each other again. As long as I live, I'll never forget how out of the goodness of his heart, the young Clarence Williams carefully looked out for my sisters and me. I was thrilled that, at long last, I could do something for him, my childhood protector.

School's Out. Now What?

When the day finally came to leave school, I picked up my diploma and left without ceremony. The building was empty except for a skeleton staff of secretaries and maintenance men. Stepping onto the street, I suddenly felt dizzy. My heart was racing, and I broke into a sweat. The heat from the hot concrete of the sidewalk radiated past the soles of my shoes, up my legs, and to my shoulders. Terrified, I was frozen in place. I didn't know the name of it, but I was having a full-fledged panic attack. For the first time, it hit me that I had nothing to show for the last six years. Feeling ill-equipped for life, I couldn't picture my future.

TURNING POINTS

CHAPTER 17

ANGELA

High school was finally over. With no game plan in mind, I took the path of least resistance that summer and worked some days for Eddie and some evenings and weekends at my father's club. I don't know if the adjectives "shy" and "flirtatious" can both be used to describe the same person, but I met a girl who fit that description in a nightclub in Queens. We hit it off right away and started dating. She was perfect. An Italian girl from The Bronx, a college graduate and student teacher. She had everything going for her except for one thing: her new boyfriend, Me. From the outset, I knew I had to set some real goals if I were to have a chance with her. I didn't want to end up like Eddie, forced by circumstances to lose the ability to plan his future. With Angela's encouragement and Eddie's support, I set my sights on broadening my opportunities.

In the fall, I registered for night school at Roosevelt High to get the necessary credits to further my education. My initial exposure to Algebra in high school was a bust, so when I got an "A" in the subject in my very first night-school class, I was shocked. I didn't fare as well in my two English classes, with no As or Bs, but I passed. "His name was Andy Duffy, and he was twenty-three, one year older than I."

Angela had just started a new student-teacher job at my old junior high, PS 45, just two blocks from Roosevelt High. She lived with her parents in a private house in an upper-middle-class neighborhood in the North Bronx. Her father was a retired New York City police detective. I was a carpenter's helper. I felt I was too far behind her and needed to catch up. She told me that if we were ever to get serious, I would have to get a city job at least. Ironically, she suggested the police department.

The Principal of PS 45, Frank G, was a neighborhood success story who often showed up at my father's club and had known Charlie Beans and me for many years. A lawyer turned teacher, then school Principal, he was now also Angela's boss and friend. After we had been seeing each other for a while, she told Frank about me. His response to her was quick and automatic,

"What are you doing with Frank Lucido? He'll never amount to anything!" While I could understand why he felt that way, I was devastated when she told me, and never forgot or forgave him. Soon after, Angela and I went our separate ways. Frank's perfunctory judgment was infuriating, and Angela's subsequent breakup with me was heartbreaking. But I definitely got the wake-up call loud and clear. Now, I was motivated. I would show them all!

I will always credit Angela with inspiring me to get off the road to nowhere I was on. Before I met her, the thought of going to college briefly crossed my mind, but I didn't really believe it could happen. College was for rich kids. That didn't stop me from asking my father if he would pay the tuition.

"Oh, that's good, Frankie. I thought only Carlo had the brains in the family. No problem, I'll cover the costs."

I was pleased to hear it, but while It sounded generous, I didn't appreciate the mixed messages. I'd always lived somewhat in the shadow of my much-loved older brother. To hear that comment all these years after Carlo's death made me feel that my father didn't think much of my intelligence.

I finished night school and limped along, making changes. Mike and Anthony were making changes, too. Mike met Roseann and married her. Anthony took his job seriously, educating himself in the liquor business. He and I broke away from our old neighborhood crowd and limited our socializing to Saturday nights to meet girls. Unlike some of my buddies, chasing girls for one-night stands wasn't for me.

At age twenty-one, I was working at the only legitimate trade I knew, carpentry. My apprenticeship with Eddie had gone as far as it could go. He taught me the basics of carpentry, but it soon became evident I had more natural talent and mechanical skills than he had. I learned all the other elements of the trade on my own. Sadly, this brilliant, self-educated man, who had been one of the very few students to receive a perfect score on his college entrance exam, was never able to go on to higher education. His father, a demanding and dictatorial parent, was a struggling cabinet maker, unable to make enough money to pay the family's bills. Eddie should have been a college professor. Instead, he had no choice but to start working full-time with his father to help support his mother and three younger siblings. Forewarned by his example, I thought it would be wise to follow Angela's advice. Go to college or get a city job.

Now, having successfully finished night school, the idea of going to college no longer fazed me. I have always been blessed with a certain dumb confidence that made me believe I could succeed at anything I chose to try. After my mother's death, the value of education was never a topic of discussion in my childhood home. My father had no interest in our schooling. When I eventually got to college, it wasn't easy. All my life, I had a great deal of difficulty in both reading and writing. Too late to help me in the **key** early years. It wasn't until much later in life that I learned there was a name for this condition, dyslexia, which was at the root of my poor behavior in school. This limitation didn't reduce my determination to acquire a college degree once I made up my mind.

My main concern at the time was about fitting into college life, which was like a foreign country to me.

CHAPTER 18

JOEL SCHREIBMAN

Still, in my early twenties, I made a new friend who changed all that for me. Charlie Velez, a friend of Anthony's and mine invited us to a party on the Upper West Side near City College. It turned out to be my first party with college kids. Entering the apartment, we were overwhelmed by how crowded it was. The place was boisterous, jam-packed with people shoulder to shoulder, loud voices and music blaring everywhere, and pot smoking. We were a couple of years older than the other guests and overdressed in our sports jackets and ties. No one noticed or cared, I'm sure. Kids were casually dressed in t-shirts and baggy jeans, some hippie types in more disheveled clothing. They floated from one to another, clicking bottles of beer, not our usual kind of crowd. I felt out of place, and it wasn't a good feeling. They met my image of college students as spoiled rich kids, smoking pot and maybe consuming other drugs or too much alcohol. I didn't smoke, especially not pot. I wasn't into this scene, but it sickened me. The three of us separated and drifted from person to person, looking for girls. I saw only the kind I wouldn't look at twice, but Anthony and Charlie wouldn't hesitate to hook up with them.

After about an hour, now bored and with no sign of my friends, I found myself in one of the bedrooms, standing at one end of a surprisingly well-built bar. The bartender offered me my first and only drink at the party—a bottle of Rheingold. I noticed one guy working his way towards the bar. He looked as out of place as I felt. With no bottle in his hand, wearing a sports jacket with an open-collared shirt, he asked for Schlitz. The bartender gave him Rheingold. I laughed and said jokingly, holding up mine,

"I asked for a Martini!" He laughed back and raised his bottle,

"Here's to your Martini!' Giving me the once over, he added,

"I'm guessing this is not your usual scene, hanging out with fraternity guys." Not knowing what a fraternity guy was and unwilling to show my ignorance, I smiled and answered,

"Dressed as you are, I could say the same about you. It takes one to know one." He grinned, admitted it was his first year in college, and introduced himself as Joel Schreibman. We quickly became good friends and spent a lot of time together that fall and winter, going to clubs and local dances and mixers. On his first spring break, he invited me to join him on a drive through the South. We ended up in Georgia, where we stayed at his aunt's spacious home while she was on vacation. We had the place all to ourselves, and I felt like a rich man living in a private home with a swimming pool and a lake with a dock. This adventure was my first vacation with a friend. Driving through several states on Route 95, making stops in Richmond, Durham, Savannah, and other historic Southern towns, opened up a new world to me. I enjoyed getting to know Joel better, and he learned a lot about me on this trip, including my petty prejudices and quirky ways of looking at things. He never passed judgment and accepted me for who I was. Because of this friendship, my view of the world first expanded beyond the narrow boundaries that had defined my youth. Recalling my hostile and judgmental attitude toward the people at the party where we met, I came to understand I needed to respect the rights of others and be more tolerant of the ways of those different from me. I had to curb my gut reactions and feelings towards those I disagreed with. Where I came from, in the closed Bronx community of Little Italy, with its restrictive codes and customs, you were either a friend or an enemy! It was a necessary lesson in changing my outlook on life.

Spring break was over, and Joel returned to college. We met a few times for drinks. In one of our last meetings, I consulted Joel about my future, looking for his advice.

"I'm from Arthur Avenue. I want something more." Joel knew I didn't want to be a carpenter all my life. Still living under my father's roof, going to college was out of the question until I could earn enough money to move out on my own. He suggested that I look for a full-time job that would earn me enough money to further my education.

When I told Eddie that I wanted to try to do something other than carpentry in order to go to college, he was excited for me and told me to follow my dreams.

CHAPTER 19

IRWIN GOLDBERG

I began to look at classified ads in The New York Times. The first one I answered was for a salesman's job in the South Bronx. Having no experience in job hunting, I chose the only Bronx ad submitted. I thought a job on my turf would be less pressure than jobs offered in Manhattan, and rejection there would be easier to handle.

Duchin Creations, located in the South Bronx, manufactured brass tables, bar carts, shelving units, and chairs. The furniture was sold in upscale stores like Macy's and Bloomingdale, as well as small specialty outlets. It was owned by relatives of the famous piano player and bandleader of the thirties and Forties, Eddy Duchin. Having no skills beyond carpentry and cutting poker games, I thought my chances of getting the job were slim to none, but I had to start somewhere. As a young man, I'd learned to dress by imitating the wise guys, wearing expensive clothing that fell off trucks. For the interview, I dressed up spiffy but not too flashy. From the approving way she looked at me, thankfully, I had made an impression on the middle-aged receptionist. So far, so good! With a warm smile, she picked up the intercom,

"Mr. Duchin, I have a young man here who answered our ad. I'm sending him in."

I was in trouble!

As it turned out, the timing was perfect. It was a family business, and the receptionist was Mrs. Duchin. They were looking for a fresh face to work with one of their salesmen. I teamed up with Irwin Goldberg, a well-spoken, well-dressed salesman who knew the ropes. We traveled all over New York State, visiting top furniture retailers, large and small. Irwin and I became good friends. He was an incredible partner and role model. Because of his patience and careful instruction, I took to the position very quickly and found I had a talent for it. I loved the job!

Irwin and his wife, Ruth, had a very young daughter, a toddler named Susan. She was his everything. He taught me how to play chess, and we had regular weekly games. I was so intrigued with the game that he let me borrow his book, "Winning Chess." After two or three months, I was able to give him real competition. My teacher no longer beat me every time.

Almost a year had passed since we were informed that Duchin Creations was moving out of state. The company offered us the opportunity to stay with them in their new location. I was tempted, but Irwin didn't want to move his family. Rosenthal, the internationally renowned makers of fine china, offered him a job representing their Thomas brand. Thomas was a line of informal, everyday dinnerware featuring simple but sophisticated modern design. Until he asked me if I wanted to work with him, I was afraid I would have to rethink my life once more. Again, Irwin took me under his wing. After familiarizing myself with the product, I took such a strong liking to the Cobalt Blue pattern that I made sure to take along a dinner plate to show customers, along with our high gloss color catalog. Irwin often teased me that I didn't have to bring my plate to dinner.

For the first two weeks, we went for training at the magnificent Rosenthal showroom on Madison Avenue. To educate us and impress interested customers, they had a handsome space reserved to demonstrate how bone china is made. We were taught how to handle and present their elegant cups, plates, and serving dishes, as well as their wine glasses, barware, and flatware, to buyers so that body oils would not dull or spot the products. I was making good money, living in a spacious studio apartment in an area of The Bronx, a far cry from my Arthur Avenue days. I had moved out of Little Italy. I was on my way!

We spent the next six or seven months servicing our company's customers and introducing the Thomas line to numerous department stores and shops throughout New York and New England. When on the road, we played chess, ate well, and might have one too many at times, but we never screwed up on the next day's business. When circulating our route back to New York City and the Long Island area, Ruth would invite me to stay for dinner once or twice a week. After our meal, Irwin always spent a few minutes playing with his beloved daughter. Then, we usually tangled in a game of chess.

One early evening, following a long day on Long Island, Irwin made us each a gin Martini before dinner. After dessert, as we made our way to the terrace that overlooked Long Island Sound, he stopped and bent over to place a tender kiss on Susan's forehead while she napped on the couch. Sipping coffee and discussing the day's successful sales results, life was good for this kid in his twenties.

After about half an hour, we heard a choking sound in the living room. Jumping out of our chairs, we found Susan gasping for air on the floor. The

911 system had not yet started in New York. Ruth frantically called the local police while Irwin tried to resuscitate Susan. Turning her on her stomach and hitting her back, he tried to dislodge whatever may have been stuck in her throat. Susan, still gasping for air, was losing color in her face just as the police rescue team arrived. They put her on a stretcher and hastily left the apartment. There wasn't enough room in the elevator for me. Obviously frightened, but trying to reassure me, Irwin managed to say,

"Frank, we're okay. Close my door and go home. I'll call you if we need you." An hour later, I phoned the hospital and learned that Susan had died from suffocation. She swallowed an olive that was left on the cocktail table where we had pre-dinner hors d'oeuvres earlier.

Irwin was never the same. He left the job and ended our friendship. The last time we spoke, he told me that he needed time to mourn, asked me not to call him and that he would be in touch with me when he was ready. After about four months, I decided to call him anyway. The phone number had been disconnected. On one of my trips back from my Long Island route, I stopped by his building in Bayside, Queens, and asked the doorman if he knew how he was doing. With sadness, the man told me that the Goldbergs had moved away over a month ago and left no forwarding address.

I was heartbroken. Irwin instilled in me a sense of confidence that stayed with me for the rest of my life. But without him, I lost all interest in selling. Every store I entered was a reminder of my dear friend. By nature, I had a cheerful demeanor and an easy smile that were great assets for the job. After Irwin's departure, they, too, were gone.

When I had to force my smiles on the buyers, my days as a salesman were over.

CHAPTER 20

MOVING ON

Back when I was working with Eddie, I'd heard about the *Chief Leader*, a newspaper focusing on New York civil service matters, which had a large Help Wanted section offering City jobs and job certifications. I began to buy the paper every week. Eddie not only encouraged me but also reminded me that it was a means to work my way through college. As summer was ending in 1965, I read that there were housing inspector openings with the Department of Buildings. The requirements were to have at least five years of experience in one of the trades of plumbing, electrical, carpentry, or construction. Another ad was for a training course in Brooklyn for the Inspector's job. I filled out the DOB application, which included my qualifications. The test would be held in four months, time enough for me to take the course. About three weeks after the test, the results were posted in The Chief, as the paper is known today. I was pleased to see my name in the top third of the class.

I remember it was a very cold day in the new year. I arrived at the Department of Buildings in Manhattan to be interviewed for the position of Housing Inspector. Along with about half a dozen other applicants, I sat in a small waiting room. To my surprise, most of the men were in their late fifties or early sixties. Only one other guy besides me was not, and we gravitated toward each other. His name was Andy Duffy, and he was twenty-three, one year older than me. The interviewer, a tall, well-built, handsome man, maybe in his mid-forties, entered the room. He introduced himself as Inspector Martinico and politely congratulated us for passing a difficult test.

With five of us left Andy was called in. After his interview, he wished us all good luck and specifically shook my hand. Looking discouraged, he said, "Good luck, Frank," and left. This was not a good sign!

My turn came. The interview room was tiny and empty except for a small desk and two chairs. Sitting uncomfortably directly across from Inspector Martinico, I could virtually stretch my arm out and touch him. While looking at my application, he asked me a number of unexpected but simple technical questions about plumbing and general construction. He then got personal.

"I see you are from The Bronx. You show two addresses on your application, one on Astor Avenue and the other on Crotona Avenue. Which one do you live at?"

"I live on Astor Avenue, off Pelham Parkway. I only added Crotona Avenue because the application asks for a prior address."

"Mr. Lucido, do you know that the requirements are five years of experience from the age of eighteen?"

"Yes, I do."

"You have several months before you meet the requirements." I knew where he was going with this and decided to roll the dice.

"Inspector Martinico, with all due respect, may I ask you a personal question?"

"Sure, go right ahead."

"What was your earliest age when you learned your trade?"

"I was in my early teens. Why do you ask?"

"I'm from Arthur Avenue! I asked because, like many Italians, I was ten years old when I started learning my trade. You looked at my face. Now look and feel my hands. You will see and feel my qualifications."

He laughed and replied,

"You're good, Mr. Lucido. I will take this under consideration."

Some time had passed, and I hadn't heard from him. I decided to put in motion my plan to further my education. I went to my father's club to ask him for the tuition he promised to give me for City College. Once again, he put me off, telling me to lay it out. This time, I got the message that he wasn't interested in my goals, and I never again asked him for financial help.

I told him I passed the Inspector's test and asked if there was anyone with a city job in the club who could help me along. He said he would check with Joe Fats. A day or two after I met with Dad, he called to tell me not to worry, "You've got the job."

Andy Duffy got the job, too, and we were subsequently reunited as Housing Inspectors in the West Harlem office. We were still the youngest on the scene and were affectionately called "The Mod Squad," after a popular TV series. The show featured young undercover cops!

In spite of this success, my father's disappointing reaction to my renewed request for help with college tuition unintentionally fired up my determination. I wanted a college degree, not just for its enrichments but to prove a point to myself.

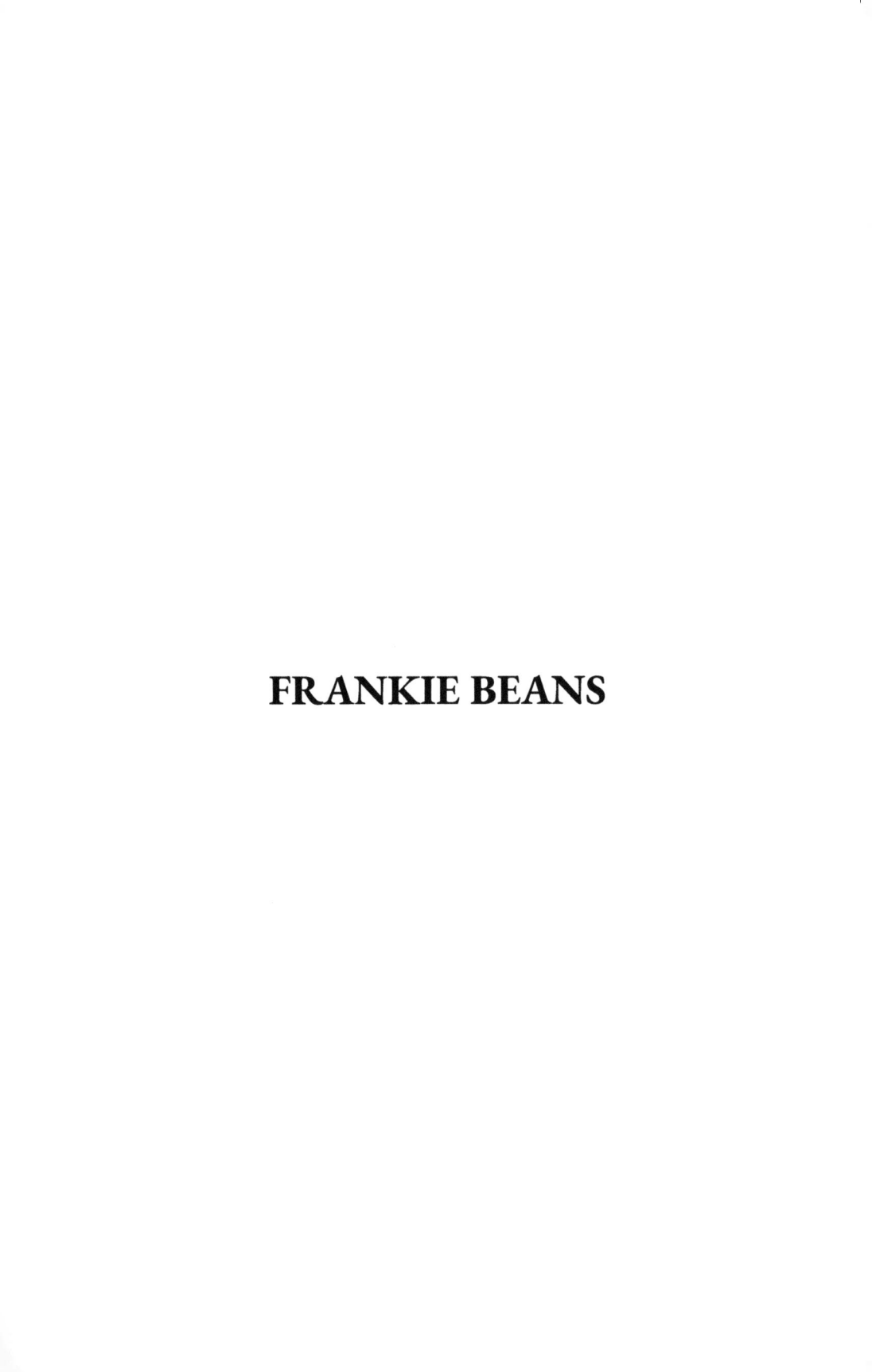

FRANKIE BEANS

CHAPTER 21
COUNTERFEITING

In my twenties, I moved out of my father's home and no longer worked in his club. But I was still the son of Charlie Beans in many ways. In fact, many of my friends called me Frankie Beans. My friend Mike had the apartment right next to mine, and after Saturday night socializing in bars and nightclubs, we often invited friends for Sunday breakfast in one of our apartments. Mike's mind was always filled with inventive schemes and scams that our friends and I were happy to go along with.

Circulating in the neighborhood at this time were counterfeit $20 bills that low-level wise guys were passing in gas stations, food stores, and restaurants around The Bronx. Mickey Morris, among others, relied on counterfeiting as one of his most lucrative illegal activities. The bills we saw were not the most professionally made fakes. Both the coloring and weight of the bill were off. My father's godson, Pauly M, who was our age and was being groomed for "the life," often ran into us in nightclubs with other guys from the neighborhood. One Saturday night, at one of our haunts, he showed Mike some $20 bills. They had

Mike Nardi

the right coloration, but the background was too white. Others had tried unsuccessfully to correct the colors, using various methods, including food coloring and even washing the bills in tea. Pauly told Mike he would be willing to pay up to three bucks per bill if he could find someone who could make them look real. Mike took the bills, and when he showed them to me in his apartment, my immediate reaction was that nothing could make them look passable. The white paper looked all wrong to my eyes.

"Forget this. I'll see you tomorrow, Mike. Breakfast in my apartment."

At about 4 am, I woke up and jumped out of bed. I was sure I found a way to make those bills pass as real! I sat and thought it through for a while, then went back to sleep. By 9 am, coffee was on. Mike came in, surprising me with our favorite bagels and lox. I couldn't wait to tell him,

"I think I found a way to color the bills! Bring a pizza tomorrow night, and I'll show you how."

He pestered me to explain, but what I had in mind, I didn't want to share with him until I was sure my formula and concoction worked. I planned to skip work the next day. Monday was an eternity for Mike. After a hurried pizza, we cleared the table, and I told him to get the $20's out. I'd color the bills, but he had to guess what was in the formula. I went into my kitchen and turned on the oven. I opened a kitchen cabinet and took out a five-inch ashtray that held a shallow liquid I had placed there. Dipping a thin artist's brush with long bristles into the liquid, I carefully began to stroke it from left to right and back again, using precisely the amount of liquid necessary. This was no job for a layman! With Mike watching closely, the white turned into the exact color of a real bill, as did the green. As gratified as I was at how correct I had been earlier in the day when I did my preliminary test, Mike was astonished. He confessed to me that he had been trying to color Pauly's bills for two weeks.

"You're a genius!"

I didn't consider myself any genius. I had taken some classes at the School of Art and Design and had done well in them, but I decided not to pursue a career in that field.

"Mike put your nose close to the ashtray and see if you recognize the smell."

"Oh shit, this is oil paint. But how did you get such a perfect color?"

"I went to an art store. I bought yellow ocher tubes, brown, green and white oil paint, and some linseed oil. I spent three hours today, with a crisp, real $20 bill in front of me, mixing colors until I settled on this one."

Together, we colored Pauly's bills and placed them in the oven at a low temperature to dry. To our surprise, "baking" the bills added a thickness and weight to them that felt like the real McCoy. Mike reminded me that Pauly would pay up to three bucks per bill. I told him that Pauly must never know that we are partners. "As far as anyone else is concerned, you are doing this on your own. And most important, it's only a one-shot deal." I reminded him what happened when Mickey Morris moved in on my father's club. I wanted nothing to do with the wise guys!

"Mike, you must give me your word that we, together and separately, make this only a one-time event. No matter how much Pauly presses you, he must understand this is a one-shot deal."

"Frankie, we've been through a lot together. Say no more."

Together, we spent the rest of the evening coloring Mike's supply of the bills. Pauly was ecstatic when he saw the samples and gave us a stack of bills to color. We needed a place to hide the finished bills as we went along. I remember a few years back. I had made a secret pocket in a small cabinet door to hide policy slips for a wise guy friend of a friend. In Mike's apartment, we were able to alter the bottoms of two hollow sliding doors to store our finished product. Months later, The New York Times ran an article about very good counterfeit $20 bills that had been circulating in The Bronx and Westchester. At the time, I found it immensely flattering and felt only a heady pride in my handiwork. Now, I can only cringe at the recollection of my short-sighted, stupid, and dangerous criminal behavior.

CHAPTER 22

PRISON TIME

Business, as usual, came back to the club after the murder. My father quickly put back his lost weight, and everything seemed the same. The increased number of wise guys dropping in did not affect the regular blue-collar workers of the neighborhood.

There existed harmony and expectation that they would be treated with the respect that they couldn't get from outsiders living in their Little Italy area. It was thought that the killing was just a regrettable thing of the past and that life would go on as usual. And it did.

Around the same time, the Federal Government began cracking down on Mickey Morris' operations. In the summer of 1966, a man in his forties, Joey S, an acquaintance of my father for well over twenty years, started showing up in the club. He became close to Dad after the killing and expressed concern about his health and emotional condition. Beans was appreciative of his attention and new friendship. One day, during lunch with my father in the club, Joey took out a phony twenty-dollar bill and showed it to him,

"Beans, have you seen these?"

"Yeah, I have. Why?"

"I have a bunch of them that I would like to unload for a price. I may be out of line asking you, but would you be interested in them?"

"You are way out of line, Joey. I'm not a wise guy. I'm a club owner!"

"I'm really sorry, Charlie. I meant no disrespect. I hope you're not angry with me."

"No, Joey, it's just not my kind of thing. I'm not like some of the guys we know." Joey nodded. "Got it. Do you mean like Sallie-boy and Pete S? I should have talked to them. Do you think they would be interested?"

"I don't know, Joey. You'd have to ask them."

About two weeks after that conversation, I received an urgent call from my father. He was at the local precinct and wanted me to come down. He had been arrested for aiding and abetting a transfer of counterfeit money!

On the day of the arrest, Joey had been in the club. It was relativity quiet, with little activity. Around two o'clock, Joey asked my father to join him in getting some fresh air and a smoke. My father thought it was a good idea. They walked up the seven steps leading to the street, and Dad wasted no time lighting up one of his thin cigars. As he bent to light it, he saw Joey walk across the street, remove an envelope from his breast pocket, and hand it to Sallie-boy, who was waiting for him. Suddenly, Crotona Avenue, between 183rd and 187th Streets, was closed off! Police cars with sirens blasting converged directly across the street from the club, in front of the building next to the one where my father lived. Uniformed officers arrested and handcuffed Joey and Sallie-boy while at the same time, doors swung open from parked cars north and south of the club entrance, and plainclothes officers grabbed my father and handcuffed him.

Everyone was told to leave the club immediately. My father's place of business was sealed shut and labeled "Crime scene."

The only other time I ever saw my father cry was when he got a phone call from my mother's doctor informing him of her death. This time, he was in court, his world turned upside down by the betrayal of a "friend." He had just found out that the treacherous Joey was an FBI informer who, for his reasons, had Dad falsely accused and set him up. My father was convicted and sentenced to jail for a year and a day.

I heard from Cousin Frank that not long after my father's conviction, his apartment had been broken into by another one of his so-called friends, who cleaned out six cases of J&B Scotch and other things of value. Cousin Frank knew who ransacked the apartment and thought I should inform Mickey Morris. He would have the guy's legs broken, for sure! No thanks. I didn't want anything to do with that man ever again in my life! Cousin Frank and I arranged for the sale of the club and the closing of the apartment.

I visited my father in prison once a month. I couldn't believe how good he looked. Trim and well-tanned, he played bocce, baseball, and chess and was also reunited with guys from his past. He was calmer and more peaceful than I'd seen him in years. He told me that, in a strange way, this was a good experience for him. When he was released from prison, he returned to the neighborhood, but he did not find much change.

After Dad's release in 1967, he lived alone for a while in a rented room on Crotona Avenue. But he saw no need to remain in New York. He decided he would return to Sicily to live out his life in Lercara Friddi, the small town of his birth. Understanding his decision, I drove him to John F. Kennedy airport (we locals were still calling it Idlewild, although it had been over three years since it was officially renamed in honor of the assassinated president). Watching him climb the portable steps from the tarmac, I couldn't help feeling sorry for him.

Maybe eight or nine months after he had settled down in the village where he was born, I received the first of two postcards. He was excited about finding his family and meeting his uncles and many cousins. A second postcard arrived about three or four months later. It was blank, except for the following: "Pick me up at Idlewild," followed by a flight number and a date and time. When that day came, Dad's plane landed and taxied to the parking area. Hoping to observe his arrival before welcoming him home, I watched from a nearby window in the terminal. As he started down the steps from the plane, we caught sight of each other and waved. Reaching the tarmac, he took a few steps toward the terminal. Suddenly stopping short, he got on his hands and knees and kissed the ground — so abruptly one or two passengers almost tripped over him. After he picked himself up, I saw several people shake his hand. I had to hear his explanation for kissing the ground.

"Dad, was the flight that bad that you were so happy to land and find yourself still living?"

"No, Frankie, I kissed the ground because I was so happy to be home."

"I thought you were going to live out your life there. What went wrong?"

"Frankie, after the first two or three months, I realized that I probably made a mistake. There was nothing going on. The only activity was walking arm and arm with other men around a fountain in a plaza. The talk would be about local politics or complaints about their wives and children; no nightclubs, no racetrack or poolrooms. There was a small club with a bocce alley and some card tables. No poker, just Italian games like we had in the club. Can you imagine me doing these boring things? I'd have to take a long trip to Palermo to have a good time. It was costly, and I'd have to stay over because of the long drive. I kissed the ground because it was like an apology for abandoning this great country. This is my home. Not Sicily."

Las Vegas

By this time, Mickey Morris had relocated to Florida. The new boss of the neighborhood was Little Phil, another old friend of my father's. Little Phil fast-tracked Dad's getting an apartment in the Mt. Carmel Center for senior citizens, newly-built for the local community in Belmont. Although people in surrounding areas were also eligible to live there, the wise guys wouldn't hear of it. Their connections with community leaders ensured only longtime residents from the neighborhood would get to occupy the apartments. Outsiders were told there was a "waiting list."

Now back in his element, Charlie Beans was running Las Vegas nights for Little Phil in The Bronx and lower Westchester. At the same time, he was busy inventing a new Las Vegas-type table game he had high hopes for. He brought it to Little Phil to get his opinion on its chances of succeeding and wondered if it would work in Vegas. Little Phil thought my father might have something viable. Through his contacts in the gambling world, he arranged an introduction to someone in Vegas who could help my father present his game to people in the know. Beans obtained a patent, and accompanied by an associate of Little Phil, set off for Las Vegas with a prototype of his game. Before he left, Dad gave me all the paperwork for his invention for safekeeping. Knowing how excited he was and his propensity to throw money around with the boys, I warned him not to go crazy when he got there. He assured me that he had plenty of money and not to worry. Maybe a week went by, and I got a call from him. Disappointed that his game wasn't accepted, he's decided to stay a few more days. Worried, I replied,

"Dad, I'm sorry it didn't work out for you. Are you okay?"

"I'm good. I took a chance. Nothing ventured, nothing gained."

"Okay, be careful and place a limit on your gambling. You know better than most the odds are in favor of the house."

"Of course, I know. Don't worry!"

A few days later, he called again and asked me to wire him $1,000 because he lost a lot at the tables. Furious, I made myself stay calm. I told him I'd send him the money, but he must promise to take the first plane home. He promised he would. Three days passed, and I was getting concerned because I hadn't heard from him. Then the phone rang.

"Frankie, I'm in a bind here. I need $5,000."

"Dad, are you kidding me? You said you'd definitely come home as soon as you received the money I wired you. You lied to me! I haven't heard from you. I thought something awful happened.

He persisted,

"Are you going to send it to me or not?"

"No, I'm not! Borrow the plane fare, and I'll reimburse you when you return. I'm hanging up!"

An hour later, he called me back.

"If you don't send me what I need, I'm committing suicide!"

This time, I hit the roof.

"How dare you try to use a son's love for his father as a threat? Do what you have to do! Goodbye!" I had never been so angry. A week later, I learned from a friend that he was back in the neighborhood. I'd seen a side of my father that had never been apparent before, and I couldn't handle it. I was disgusted by his attempt at emotional blackmail, and it created a rift that could have been permanent. Nine months later, I got a call from his half-sister, my Aunt Frances, who lived in New Jersey. He had stayed in touch with her all his life and was on good terms with her. I remember her and her family fondly. She told me he was heartbroken and wanted to apologize to me. She implored me to patch things up. I told her if he agreed not to say a word to me about what happened in Vegas, I would meet with him. He was working at one of Little Phil's clubs, and I met him there. We hugged and kissed each other. He whispered in my ear,

"I'm so sorry."

"You buying the drinks?" I asked him with a smile.

CHAPTER 23

NOT YET ON THE STRAIGHT AND NARROW

Being raised in an environment where double-dealing was a way of life, it's not surprising that Mike and I each had a streak of creative larceny. Our fathers — his a house painter and part-time bookie, mine a barber turned club owner — were not the greatest role models.

Jimmy the Thief

One of the colorful characters we knew was Jimmy the Thief, a guy around our age who moved around the neighborhood selling stolen goods. He had all kinds of great stuff, like small stereos and cameras, but specialized in high-end men's clothing. Naturally, my buddies and I used his services. Impressive looking at six-foot-two, slim of build, he was always perfectly tailored and well-spoken. He'd have us go into Sulka, one of the most famous luxury men's clothing stores in Manhattan, to pick out the suits, slacks, and sweaters we wanted to own. He had his way of getting the exact items we wanted in the sizes we needed. He was our kind of personal shopper! He had lockers at Grand Central Station, where he kept his loot. He'd sell it to us for one-third the market price. Needless to say, we were happy to take advantage of his special skills.

The Original Wedding Crashers

Mike and I were a natural team. With two other close friends, we used to hang out in clubs in Manhattan, The Bronx and Queens, and in Westchester County. In Manhattan, a number of clubs were operated by the Mob, and we seldom had a problem getting into even the most popular places, so we usually avoided paying the cover charges. Thanks to our Bronx credentials, we always knew someone covering the door or had a name to mention.

One night in 1966, the four of us were driving on Northern Boulevard on our way to a nightclub in Queens. As we approached a large catering hall,

Leonard's of Great Neck, I came up with the idea of stopping there first. We'd pretend we were guests and eat and drink at the cocktail hour for free. Anthony, sitting in the back, was skeptical,

"It'll never work. We'll get caught!"

But Mike's eyes lit up immediately. "No problem," he replied. "We're probably dressed better than any of the guests. Here's what we do. We walk in, two at a time, and go directly to the buffet table or the bar. Anyone who comes near you and starts to chat, be friendly. You say to them, *Wow, this is a really nice spread*! If it's a wedding reception, you should ask them if they're friends of the groom or friends of the bride. They will most likely tell you which, so you tell them the opposite and then move on. Always be the one to ask first. As usual, Mike's input carried the day. We tried out our plan that evening, and it was a total success. On weekend nights, sampling the catering halls became our routine before hitting the clubs.

In a Scarsdale nightclub one time, we met two Jewish guys who were friends from college, Harold R. and Morty L. We hit it off with Harold right away. He had the mindset of someone who might have grown up in our neighborhood. He liked our style. We weren't big drinkers, but we looked sharp and had a sense of fun. As the evening progressed, Harold complimented us on how we dressed and asked us where we got such nice clothing. Discovering he was unfamiliar with the phrase "It fell off a truck," we taught him a few choice expressions and a little bit about how we lived. He was very interested in knowing more. We explained things don't actually "fall off" trucks. They were highjacked goods available to us through contacts in our old neighborhood. From then on, he would often join us on our nights out and participate in our delinquent behavior. He was now one of our crew. Morty came along for the ride once in a while.

At that time, Anthony was sharing my apartment, working in a liquor store during the day while attending college at night. He started complaining that we were not meeting upscale girls. When he brought the topic up with our group in a club one night, Harold told him we're not going to find educated girls in places like these. He suggested we might like to go up to the Catskill Mountains when the Concord and other resort hotels had Singles weekends — noting the guests were predominantly Jewish, but some non-Jews also attended these special weekends. The only problem was that you couldn't get into the parking lot without a bona fide reservation. I chimed in with,

"That's a great idea. I lived up in the area when I was younger and visited all the famous hotels — the Concord, Grossinger's, the Raleigh — several times with my father. I even saw Rocky Marciano training at Grossinger's." We left off that I would speak to Morty and ask him to look into the cost involved in going to a Singles weekend. Morty told me it wouldn't be cheap. We learned the prices ranged from $70 to $115 a day per room, including three meals. A minimum two-night stay was required for those weekends. I came up with an idea for our six-man crew, and Mike created a workable scheme.

The Scheme

Morty and I would make a reservation for an Executive Suite in both our names and ask for confirmation to be sent to each of us individually. This spacious accommodation included two very large beds, convertible couches, and a variety of luxurious features. The total price for the suite for the two nights was $230. Having copies of the reservation sent to each of our addresses would allow two cars to pass through the gatehouse leading to the hotel parking lot. Three people drive up in each car. A few minutes from the hotel, we would pull off to the side of the road, and one person would hide in the trunk. Once in the parking lot, the third person was able to exit the trunk completely unnoticed. All six of us now had access to the hotel. Each of us needed a meal ticket to get into the dining room, where we could all gorge on three sumptuous meals a day. The reception desk was maybe fifty feet long and crowded with check-ins. Morty and I would separate and check in at different ends of the crowded counter. Showing our respective reservations, we each requested two meal tickets, claiming our roommates would be coming up later in the evening. We now had four meal tickets and our room assignment. Mike would take one of our reservations in case he needed to show one, but he was such a natural performer. All he had to do was tell one of the desk clerks that someone told him he needed a meal ticket and probably one for his roommate. Never challenged, most of the people behind the desk were unsuspicious students with summer jobs. We were home free!

Each night after dinner, the guests ended up at the nightclub where there was always name entertainment. Mike wasn't a handsome man and was usually timid with women. But he was gifted with an unbelievable memory for jokes and was capable of physically mimicking any accent or action the joke demanded. In that way, he was a magnet to the ladies. Mixing with women at the bar, where he was his own 'show, he carefully watched how certain women paid their bills. He would single out women who carelessly signed bar tabs without checking the charges. Mike specifically observed the way they wrote their signatures. He looked for those who signed with just an initial followed by their last name. Remarkably, there were several such women. Mike memorized some names and room numbers as they left the bar. From that point on, our drinks and table wine were 'compliments' to these ladies.

One weekend, while I was watching Mike standing in line to pay our bill, he surreptitiously caught my eye and pointed to the woman in front of him. Hers was one of the signatures he had most used during our stay. It was Barbara Gold who signed her bills as B. Gold. He wasn't overly concerned about the outcome if she learned her signature had been forged, but was curious to see her reaction once she saw her total bill. When she reached the window to pay, he could read the final bill when it was handed to her; it was over $400. To Mike's surprise, she took out her checkbook and paid it, no questions asked. When it was our turn to check out, our total bill, when divided by the six of us, amounted to a mere $40 per person for the whole three-day weekend.

CHAPTER 24

"MAFIA! MAFIA! MAFIA!" (I START A RENT STRIKE)

The attractive Astor Avenue building where Mike N and I lived in 1968 was built and managed by two Italian men who had recently sold it to a wealthy real estate family who owned some seventy-five to eighty apartment buildings in New York City. These people, the Steins, had a bad reputation. As landlords, they failed to fulfill their obligations to tenants, cutting corners and avoiding making necessary repairs; because of this, when my apartment was due for a paint job, as called for in my lease, I thought it best if I did all the work myself. I called their office to remind them that it was time for my studio to be painted and offered to do the job if they would give me the paint. The person I spoke to agreed. Figuring I would be given four or five gallons of paint, I drove my car down to their office in Manhattan and parked in a nearby garage.

The Steins' office was a large storefront with two aisles of desks and what looked like a dozen employees. The receptionist directed me to the head of the firm's office in the back. Entering that room, I saw Harvey Stein and his expensively dressed wife, Sadie Stein.

"Hello, Mr. Stein, I'm Frank Lucido from 789 Astor Avenue in The Bronx. I was told to see you regarding picking up the paint for my apartment."

He had a blank, uninterested look on his face. Before he could utter a word, Sadie jumped in,

"We don't paint apartments." Her husband then spoke,

"Vee don't paint apartments, but I give you paint."

Bending down, he reached under his desk, pulled out a quart of white paint, and placed it in front of me.

Smiling in disbelief, I said,

"Go on, Harvey, you're only kidding, right?"

"I don't kid. Dis is vut I give," he said again.

Sadie then piped up,

"You're lucky he gave you this!"

"Mr. Stein, I drove all the way down here, parked my car in a garage, and I'm not leaving here without a few gallons of paint."

"Dis is vut I give," he said again.

Pissed off but controlled and no longer smiling, I said to him,

"Harvey, be reasonable and give me the paint. You're insulting me." Without batting an eye, he repeated flatly,

"Dis is vut I give."

Controlling my anger, I replied coldly,

"Mr. Stein, for the last time, I'm asking you for the paint I need for my apartment.

I'm leaving here as a friend or as an enemy, and I'm telling you, you don't want me as an enemy!"

Jumping up from his chair, he shouted at the top of his lungs,

"Mafia! Mafia! Mafia!"

That was enough for me. I quietly turned around and walked out of that office with every intention of showing him exactly what kind of an enemy I could be. A plan immediately formed in my mind.

Well aware that my fellow tenants on Astor Avenue were unhappy with the Steins' management, I spent several days going from apartment to apartment, getting signatures to form a rent strike, and received an overwhelming vote to proceed. I found a firm of professional rent strike organizers with whom we placed the rent monies in escrow. I then looked up every piece of real estate owned by the Stein organization. I was working as a building inspector at the time, and through my contacts with the Department of Buildings, I arranged to have a Cellar to Roof inspection of every Stein-owned building. It netted well over a thousand violations, which the Steins promptly received. I had several conversations with Sadie Stein about our rent strike, but she didn't budge. Not knowing I was an Inspector, she thought I had made a ton of anonymous citizens' complaints against her buildings and threatened me with lawsuits. She was extremely unpleasant, haughty, and condescending.

In those days, our mailboxes were inundated with countless direct mail solicitations. I wanted to annoy the Steins in any way I could and came up with an idea to drive them nuts. I would fill out all kinds of offers for magazines, newspapers, car and home improvement loans, etc. I filled them out in the names of Sadie, Harvey, their son, and other members of the family, as well as for the Stein organization itself. Mike loved the idea and jumped right in on it, making sure many of the guys from the old neighborhood also filled out any offers they received, plugging in the Stein family names.

After a few months of our troublemaking, Sadie had enough. She instructed her son Izzy to bring the strike to an end and do whatever was necessary to get rid of me. He made sure all the repairs were made and that all the apartments that were due for paint jobs were covered. When all was completed and the tenants were satisfied, he asked me what it would take for me to leave the building. I told him that in order for me to disappear, he had to pay the rent strike organizers' fee, release Mike and me from our leases, and cancel both our accrued rents.

LIVING A NORMAL LIFE

CHAPTER 25

SETTLING DOWN

Aside from the fun of getting something for nothing, Anthony and I felt that the Singles weekends at the hotels in the Catskills offered us opportunities to meet the kind of women we were seeking. On one visit to the Concord, we met two wholesome Jewish girls. Both were from well-off families, one from Brooklyn and the other from Long Island. We started double-dating. When their parents inquired if the boys they were interested in were Jewish, both girls answered, "I think so." Young men in their communities were not usually named Anthony or Frank, and I was sure all four parents were hoping these fellows would be passing fancies. They weren't. Over the objections of both sets of parents, these two nice Jewish girls married the two Italian boys from The Bronx.

It was 1973. I was still attending Baruch College at night while working a steady job as a New York City Building Inspector. My in-laws-to-be were somewhat relieved when I agreed that our children would be raised in the Jewish faith. We married and had a small reception with close friends and family at a hotel in Brooklyn. Charlie Beans had a very good time with my father-in-law's brother, another gambler who also knew his way around the ponies. Ultimately, I was accepted when my son Paul was born, and I followed through on my promise to raise him in the Jewish faith. With a gift from my wife's parents and the proceeds from the sale of some property I owned in The Bronx, we purchased a home in East Rockaway, in the affluent Five Towns area on Long Island.

In 1975, I'd been a Building Inspector for almost ten years, had a newborn baby boy and a house with a mortgage, and my BBA degree from Baruch College was finally within reach. As luck would have it, that year coincided with New York City's financial crisis, and suddenly I was out of a job. The Buildings Department laid off all inspectors who had fewer than eleven years of service. My father-in-law was a certified public accountant and lawyer. Since I had majored in accounting at Baruch, where I'd also studied the CPA curriculum, he offered to train me in field auditing until I figured out what to do with my life. I spent a few weeks working with him and found it boring. I didn't like sitting at a desk looking at numbers all day long.

CHAPTER 26

"MY MIND SAYS YES, BUT MY HEART SAYS NO"

An idea came to me that maybe I could work for Eddie in a management capacity. During most of the past decade, while I was with the Buildings Department, I had devoted one week of my four-week vacation to managing his business. This allowed him to take a short vacation. He always had plenty of work but wore himself out because of the time-consuming and obsessively repetitive method he used to keep track of his orders. When I called to discuss my Idea with him, he was excited and happy to hear from me. Before I could bring up the subject, he asked me to meet him for lunch the following Saturday.

When the day came, I met him at his new shop on Jerome Avenue. The place was his usual unholy mess. There wasn't an inch of space to spare. Pieces of wood and moldings were strewn all around, and large storage bins along a side wall, holding windows and other things, were inaccessible. To reach any part of the shop, you had to work your way through a series of narrow pathways. Eddie's desk was cluttered with papers, along with the lined notebooks he used instead of proper work orders. He was forced to spend seven days a week at his business, primarily due to his lack of basic organizational skills. I had repeatedly tried to convince him to allow me to make changes that would free up his time. My suggestions fell on deaf ears.

Over lunch, it turned out Eddie was way ahead of me! He started the conversation with a direct question,

"Frank, since you are free from the Buildings Department, how do you feel about being my partner?" I was floored by the offer and needed time to think about it. I knew one thing for sure — there was no way I could partner with him the way he was used to running things.

"Eddie, after all these years, it would be natural for us to be partners. The only problem is that I would have to make some fundamental changes to keep it going as a viable operation. This would require sacrifices on your part."

"What sacrifices must I make, Frank?"

"First, a total revamping of the shop. Every item must have its place, not scattered around as it is now. The shop must be cleaned of all debris. You have opened cartons of expensive new locks and other hardware that have been used just for parts, a waste of money. And most importantly, there must be a modern work order system. If you are willing to make the changes, I will set it all up myself."

He agreed. The thought of a written contract of partnership never entered my mind. He was like family to me. After two months of backbreaking work, the place was in ship shape. I created simple work order forms in triplicate, taking all the open jobs and writing out tickets for each — one copy for the men, one for our records, and one for daily routes to be pinned up on a cork board I hung in the office. The workers liked the changes and were getting used to the new system. Eddie wasn't happy that the tickets were loose, and he had a hard time adjusting to the new ways.

About six months into our partnership, while having lunch together, he looked at me from across the table. Tears filled his eyes, and he said to me,

"My mind says yes, but my heart says no. Frank, I can't have a partner." I didn't try to argue with him and managed to keep my emotions under control. We separated amicably, but I was also very angry with my old friend. There wasn't the slightest doubt in my mind that I could have tripled and quadrupled the business. It was growing, and if he didn't make changes, one day, he would suffer physically or emotionally from the inevitable strain. Sadly, his inflexibility created a missed opportunity for both of us.

The very first thing I did was to order the Sunday New York Times to be delivered each week to my home. When my wife asked me why, I told her,

"It's only a matter of time before Eddie puts an ad in the newspapers to sell his business, and I will be the first to answer that ad.

CHAPTER 27

ESTABLISHING A BUSINESS

I started my own carpentry business. One lucky day, in response to my ad for a carpenter, I received a phone call from an out-of-work Dominican cabinet maker, Roberto Landeta. I interviewed him, and it was apparent he was overqualified for the position. I hired him on the spot.

In the mid-1960s, I made my first real estate investment in The Bronx, a piece of property on Allerton Avenue. It consisted of two small buildings that contained both commercial space and apartments. One of my tenants, Violet Wasserman, who impressed me with her take-charge manner, agreed to cover the phones in exchange for a temporary reduction in rent. She eventually became a full-time paid employee.

By 1978, I had three vans and five mechanics in the field. The owner of one of my competitors, 'Held 300,' wanted to sell his company and asked me if I was interested. The price was right, and I was happy to buy him out. At this time, I was "sharing" a number of accounts with Eddie's Bettermade Woodworking.

Webster Avenue was mostly residential, and indoor parking spaces weren't available for my vans. They were parked on the street, and often over the weekends, one or two of them were vandalized, a nuisance I had to do something about.

By a stroke of luck, another opportunity came my way I couldn't ignore. The owner of Hausmann Service Corporation had passed away, and his top manager was ready to retire. The man approached me on behalf of Mr. Hausmann's widow, and I was soon under contract to buy out my biggest competitor! Hausmann's business was housed in a 15,000-square-foot commercial building at Inwood Avenue and 170th Street. It had a fully-equipped shop that made mine look like the minor leagues, along with two vans in excellent condition. I kept their three remaining carpenters and put all my field men in uniforms. Solving another problem, the building's garage could easily accommodate ten vans plus one car, which my foreman used to inspect jobs throughout lower Westchester, The Bronx, and Manhattan.

The expanded business called for two secretaries to answer the phones and do the billing. I made sure to keep both the original phone numbers and had one secretary answer the Residential Repair phone and the other handle Hausmann's calls. Potential clients almost always called both companies for estimates. I always priced one job higher than the other, just about guaranteeing we got the job!

The Madonna Saves the Day

Meanwhile, Anthony and his business partner, a mutual friend of ours from The Bronx, had three giant liquor stores, two in Brooklyn and one in Manhattan. Anthony was able to buy a million-dollar mansion formerly owned by a member of the Gucci family. It was on seven acres, with a groundskeeper, in Westchester County.

He had many elaborately catered parties in one of the great rooms of his home. I noticed that very few of our old crowd were invited. Most of his new friends were well-heeled locals with nothing in common with the people he grew up with. Knowing our old neighborhood's association with the Mafia, many of these people were captivated by Anthony, believing he was somehow "connected." Not all, but some of his guests were obnoxious — interrupting conversations, bragging about their material possessions, unashamedly flattering their host.

On one hot spring day, nine years later, he invited my second wife and me to spend the day at his home and enjoy his pool. After dinner, he told me he sold two of his acres to a developer and asked if I wanted to see the property. It was beautifully landscaped, surrounded by a forested area. In the distance, I noticed a row of newly- planted small trees spaced about six feet apart.

"What's with those trees? Is that the boundary of your property?"

"Yeah, can you believe this? This fucking developer builds million-dollar homes, and this is what he gives me as screening. I'm so pissed off. Also, look how close that house is to my property."

"Didn't you have it in your contract for some type of screening?"

"I did. I had a choice of a fence or trees. I didn't want an unsightly fence, so I chose trees. When I saw them planting these twigs, I complained that they were too small and that I didn't want to see that large house. He told me that he was only required to plant trees, and these are trees. I was thinking of going down to the neighborhood to see if I could get somebody to straighten his ass out!"

It didn't take me more than a split second to state with confidence,

"I can straighten this out for you."

"Frank, this is not the kind of thing you should get involved with."

"I'm not getting involved with this at all. You'll do the whole thing! Do as I say, and you will have your proper screening in no time. Do you have a hardware store in this town?"

"Yeah, in Bedford. Why?"

"What I'm about to tell you is that you probably won't have to do once you tell the builder your intentions. But if he puts you off, this is what you do. Remember where Jackie Cipolla lived on 187th Street?"

"Yes, above the candy store."

"Good. Across the street is the religious store. Go in and buy a 3' Madonna statue. From your hardware store, buy four clothes poles and 100' of nylon clothesline. Take the Madonna and place it a few feet from your lot line. Place the poles in the ground 8' apart. Then, string the clothesline along the poles. After you set this up, pin-stained garments, underwear, towels, and cotton dresses are along the line. I guarantee you that the builder will replace every tree!"

A week later, Anthony called to tell me that he was watching fully-grown pine trees being planted.

"Give me any date. We're taking you and your wife to the finest restaurant in New York by limo."

Mutual Love

One Sunday, as I had done every Sunday since Eddie called off our partnership, I opened the business opportunities section of The New York Times. There it was: "Business for sale," with Eddie's phone number. Unwilling to get Eddie on the phone directly, I wanted to feel him out through his wife Claire, so I had my wife call her. Their conversation was cordial, and Claire was very receptive to my interest in buying his business. Eddie was out, taking his morning walk, and she suggested I call him in an hour. He was happy to hear my voice, and we had a very friendly talk with no mention of our past problems. We arranged to meet at my office to talk over what each of us had in mind. He was very agreeable, and we set a date and time.

At our first meeting, he was completely honest with me, telling me that what I predicted came to be. He had recently recovered from a nervous breakdown. His seven employees were robbing him, cheating on time in the field, and stealing expensive hardware from his shop and fuel from his vans. His customers were giving him less work because he couldn't get the jobs done on time. Much of that work had already started coming my way. He was humble and very sad that his "baby," Bettermade Woodworking, was dying. We scheduled our lawyers to meet with us at my shop in two weeks.

On the appointed date, accompanied by my wife, I was at my office an hour early in order to get a start on my business day. Both lawyers soon followed. From my office window, I could see the slow, deliberate walk of a broken man, walking hand in hand with his wife. Eddie and Claire made their way to the front door and up the few steps to my office. Eddie was pale and sat quietly. Just after his lawyer began to talk, I interrupted him and said,

"Excuse me," and turned to Eddie.

"Eddie, do you mind if you and I step out for a minute?"

Sitting there, looking at my lifelong friend and mentor, I was suddenly filled with emotion and felt a pressing need to share my thoughts with him. I helped him down the steps onto the sidewalk, taking his arm as we walked toward the corner.

"Eddie, you spent a lifetime building your business and taught me the trade. If not for you, neither of us would be here today. Maybe you don't want to retire?"

"Frank, what do you mean?"

"Eddie, do you want to be my partner?"

"Frank, do you mean what you are saying?"

"Of course I do!" Suddenly, the color came to his face.

He beamed, and his whole body language changed as he turned to face me,

"Yes, Frank. Yes! I can't believe this. I never wanted to retire. My business grew, but I didn't."

"Okay, Eddie. Then it's settled. We'll be partners. My only condition is that I will have the controlling interest in the company."

"Frank, I leave everything up to you!"

"Okay, Eddie. Let's go back, and you make the announcement." When we got back to the entrance to my office, I gave him the right of way. A newly energetic man walked up the

Claire and Eddie Borkowsky, with Violet Wasserman

steps. Entering my office with a smile on his face, he raised both arms in the air, triumphantly exclaiming to all,

"We are partners!" Then, immediately addressing the lawyers,

"Draw up the papers!" Instantaneously, everyone in the room applauded, including Violet, my secretary, who was present in our small office throughout the morning. Shouts of congratulations rang out at the unexpectedly swift resolution. The timing was perfect. Eddie had three vans and about one month after our official merger, we had all settled into the Hausmann building, which had a total of eight vans and fourteen employees. Eddie was pleased and chose to work as a field estimator for our new business. We had a perfect partnership at last!

Within a year, he began to show signs of aging. He was slowing down and was having problems walking up the stairways in the buildings we serviced. In our contract, there was a clause, suggested by Claire, that I would determine his retirement date and buy him out when that time came. By February 1981, our business had grown considerably. We had thirty employees and more than a dozen vans. Eddie's health was showing signs of weakness, and after conferring with him and Claire, we all agreed that he would retire that December. At his retirement party, he and Claire quietly called me aside to tell me that they would forgo the buy-out payments. I questioned that surprising statement,

"Why are you telling me this? You are entitled to your retirement money." Claire replied,

"Frank, you paid us in full the day we met in your Webster Avenue storefront."

Satisfaction!

A good number of years had passed. I'd finally made it. It was a success! At a function where one of our close friends was receiving an award, Frank G. was sitting a few tables away, and we nodded to each other in recognition. Encountering him at the bar when I was getting a drink, we exchanged hellos. He asked how I was doing. I looked straight into his eyes and tapped the center of my chest firmly with two fingers as my answer came pouring out,

"Frank, *this* Frank, who you once told a mutual friend would never amount to anything, spent nine years as a New York City Building Inspector, earned a business degree from Baruch College, built a business that has thirty-two employees, eleven vans, and services the real estate trade throughout the city and lower Westchester. *That's* how I'm doing!" I picked up my drink, stirred it, left the plastic swizzle stick on the counter, and walked past him as if he never existed. At last, I'd achieved satisfaction for the long-simmering vendetta in my soul!

CHAPTER 28

SCENES FROM EDDIE'S ALBUM

One hot summer day in 1957, we were finishing installing shelving for a judge in an office building on 149th Street. We were tired, and I was happy that it was the last stop of the day. When we arrived back at the shop, Eddie told me we had an emergency call at Claremont Parkway. He had me put a shovel and flashlight into his Chevy station wagon. I thought to myself, we never used a shovel in our work. What kind of emergency are we going to?

On the corner of Claremont Parkway and Third Avenue was a Bronx chain store, Spotless Dry Cleaning. After parking the car, Eddie told me to bring the flashlight and the shovel into the store as he ran ahead. When I entered the store, Eddie was yelled at by the manager. She was a big, overweight woman who had a mouth that would embarrass a sailor.

"I don't care what time it is. You should have been here hours ago! If you don't get rid of this smell today, I'm not coming back to this store, and I can guarantee you, you won't be getting work from this organization anymore."

"Madam, I'm sorry, but we were working on another job and just picked up the message."

"Well, don't just stand there, get to work. There is a terrible smell coming from under that fucking window platform, so get going!"

Popular at the time, this kind of raised interior platform ran about fifteen feet along the front of the store. It was used primarily to display advertising placards. Eddie bent down to unscrew the first of the platform's four decorative wood panels. He then told me to take the flashlight and shovel, crawl through the opening, and work my way through to see if there was a dead animal. I wiggled my way into the 'narrow, head-first channel, holding the shovel in one hand and the flashlight in the other. About halfway down, I saw a large dead rat. I scooped it into the extended shovel and then backed up by wedging my elbows into the dirt surface to exit the space. Eddie immediately disposed of the rat, replaced the panel, and ignored the manager's loud barking.

"God damn it! I knew there was a dead rat in there. You should have been here hours ago." Eddie and I silently made our exit.

I Know That Smell

Twenty-two years later, I had my own growing carpentry business that serviced the real estate trade exclusively. I had four vans and ten employees. My office was built above the lumber storage area of my shop. My secretary of three years, Violet Wasserman, was an expert communicator with a strong voice. She skillfully handled the dozens of service calls from landlords and tenants that came in daily. One winter morning, when I arrived at my office, I found her waiting for me in a state of urgency and anger. I asked her,

"Vi, what's wrong? Are you okay?"

"I can't stay here. There's a dead rat on the floor. It's been here a while, and until you find it and remove it, consider me terminated. I'm leaving!"

"Vi, I work alongside you every day. I don't smell anything."

She put her coat on, picked up her purse, and headed to the stairs. With the phones ringing behind me, I followed her to the street.

"Vi, come on. Come back to the office to talk it over."

"No, and this is final!"

I convinced her to have a cup of coffee with me at the nearby luncheonette before taking her bus home. She agreed to have coffee but insisted she wouldn't change her mind. Sitting in a booth with coffee in front of us, she kept rambling on about smells and rats and dead animals. It got to a point where I was now really fed up and was tempted to fire her on the spot. I interrupted her tirade.

"I don't smell anything. Who made you an expert on smells?"

"Don't try and snow me. I know that smell. I was once a manager for a chain store and was willing to quit over a rat smell that stunk up the shop!"

Suddenly, I sat back. I couldn't believe what I was hearing and quickly interrupted her,

"Was It on Claremont Parkway?"

Surprised, she said, "Yes!" How do you know this?"

Ignoring her question,

"You waited a long day until a carpenter and his helper finally arrived at the store.

You angrily ordered them to get to work, and the carpenter had the boy enter the window cavity to find and remove a dead rat."

"Who told you this? My sister-in-law?"

"No, Vi, I knew the boy helper who squeezed through the narrow window box. That boy was me." I could see she was stunned. Before she could say anything, I assured her I would check out her complaint as soon as I got back to the shop and said,

"I know you have a nose for that sort of thing!"

There was, indeed, a dead rat under the office floor, and Vi came back to work the next day.

An Accidental Phone Call

Eddie and Claire took their first European vacation. When they returned, I met with Eddie for lunch to get a recap. He couldn't wait to tell me he had just had one of the most rewarding experiences of his life in England.

While in London, late one afternoon, Eddie decided he had enough sightseeing. While Claire was visiting a large library, he sat outside on one of its many wide steps. Bored while sitting there, he stared at the red telephone booth near the bottom of the steps. His mind drifted back to World War II when he was a young American soldier stationed in England. He recalled his first love, a young English girl named Penelope White. Admitting to himself it was a crazy idea, he decided to look up the young British lady. From inside the booth, he consulted the hanging telephone directory, turning to the *'W'* pages. Running his fingers through the many listings under the name White, he randomly chose one of several entries with the name "*White, P*" and dialed the number. The phone rang several times before a man picked up,

"Hello."

Eddie began to speak,

"Hello, my name is....." Before he was able to complete his greeting, he was interrupted by the excited voice on the other end of the line,

"Eddie, is this you? Eddie Borkowsky?"

Astonished, Eddie answered,

"Yes, but how do you know my...?"

In a British accent, without allowing Eddie to continue, the man hurriedly asked, "Are you the American, Eddie Borkowsky, who was stationed here during the war? Eddie, you are calling for Penelope White. I know this is you! We have heard so much about you over the years from my sister, Penelope. I am her brother, Peter." Eddie couldn't get a word in. Peter eagerly went on,

"Eddie, you must come to visit us! Penelope has a Bed and Breakfast overlooking the Cliffs of Dover. She and her family will so much want to see you!" Eddie immediately agreed to visit Penelope, who was married to a former British soldier. Peter made the arrangements for himself, his wife, and Eddie and Claire to meet with Penelope. When the day of the visit arrived, Eddie looked at himself in the mirror with disdain as Claire adjusted his tie.

"Look at me. I'm a bald, freckled old man. She's expecting someone who no longer exists. I'm frightening!"

"Honey, you're so wrong. She will see her first love as handsome as ever, no matter what number of years has passed."

Humbly, he shrugged his shoulders and thanked his wife.

Their taxi pulled up to Penelope's home. They stepped out and walked to the picket fence, and Eddie opened the gate to allow Claire to pass. As they walked up the stone path, the door to the house flew open, and Penelope rushed out, arms outstretched to welcome them, her husband close behind. Claire released her arm from Eddie's and stopped to make sure Eddie would be in front of her when the two former lovers met. Penelope embraced him warmly, then pulled back and grasped his shoulders, saying,

"Eddie, how good it is to see you after all these years. You haven't changed a bit!"

At this happy reunion, Eddie and Penelope's husband discovered they had more than one thing in common. Both men had served in the armed forces during the war and struck up an immediate bond. This unplanned meeting was the beginning of a trans-ocean friendship. Penelope and her husband visited Eddie and Claire and stayed at their apartment on Mosholu Parkway in The Bronx. The Borkowskys made two subsequent visits to England and stayed at Penelope's bed and breakfast.

CHAPTER 29

TANGLING WITH MR. HAROLD LITTLE PHIL SORTS IT OUT

In 1995, no longer married to my first wife, I was living with my second wife and our young son in Westchester County. That summer, my wife wanted to rent a cabana at the Eldorado Beach Club in New Rochelle, where some of our friends and neighbors who had children my son's age were members. I was recovering from a bleeding ulcer brought on by the pressures of work, and the idea was appealing. On my first visit, we explored the club thoroughly. One of the things I liked about the particular cabana we chose was that it not only overlooked the large swimming pool but it also had a great view of Long Island Sound. Each cabana was designed to be shared with another family and had a movable partition that divided the space. Renting one usually meant occupying only half a cabana. Against my wife's initial objections, I had my eye on the coveted corner cabana at the raised area in the last row, close to the exit. She felt that its premium location was an unnecessary extra expense for us. Compounding the issue, I wanted to rent the entire cabana for some privacy. I was weakened by my recent hospital stay and preferred being by myself while she and both my boys took advantage of all the amenities the club had to offer. When she understood my reasoning, she agreed.

We were interviewed by the manager, "Mr. Harold," whose rough manner was at odds with the upscale feel of the place. He had a "take it or leave it" attitude, which I could understand as the place was very popular. On our first day at the El Dorado, we brought beach toys and other items to make the cabana home-like. Unlocking the padlock I installed when we signed the contract, I opened the door and noticed that there was only one lounge chair and one beach chair inside. Believing it was just an oversight, I had one of the cabana boys bring us another pair of chairs. We finished our decorating and began our summer at the club. My visits would be limited because of the demands of my work, but my wife was there most of the week. On my second visit, I was surprised to find only one pair of chairs. I wondered, Who has our key?" I never gave a duplicate to anyone. And why are two chairs missing again? I asked the boy how anyone could enter the cabana when I was the only one with a key. He shrugged, and after he brought us another set of chairs, he told me he didn't know what had happened and that I should talk to Mr. Harold. I spoke to someone in the management office who didn't know anything about it but promised to send Mr. Harold to me as soon as he came in. Around noon, Mr. Harold came by, obviously annoyed,

"You wanted to see to me?"

"Mr. Harold, I don't understand why the second set of chairs disappeared from my cabana."

He told me it was he who had taken the chairs. I asked him how he got into my cabana since I was the only one with a key. He said that he removed the pins from the hinges on the door to gain entry. My jaw dropped.

"That's pretty extreme, isn't it?"

"These are the rules. You're only allowed one set of chairs for each cabana." As tactfully as I could, I said,

"You didn't have the right to come into my personal space."

"Read your contract. We can enter any cabana to inspect it for any reason."

"But I rented the entire cabana."

"It doesn't matter. You get only one set of chairs."

"Mr. Harold, aren't we being a bit unfair? It's only two chairs we're talking about."

"These are the rules," he repeated, not budging. Out of patience, I raised my voice for the first and only time.

"If I would have known this, I would have never joined this fucking club!"

"You can leave anytime you want, but we will only refund 50% of your membership."

"We're only in our second week. If anything, you should charge me for the two weeks we were here."

He was emphatic.

"That's the way it is!"

He walked away. I was beside myself. I was so upset that my stomach started to burn.

By 5:00 pm that afternoon, I was home, having a drink on my deck with a neighbor, telling him what happened earlier in the day when my phone rang. It was my father calling to see how I was feeling. Mickey Morris had moved to Florida, and Charlie Beans was now organizing card games and

Las Vegas Nights for his successor on the club scene, a wise guy known as "Little Phil." I told Dad that I should be feeling okay, but I was not because I had an upsetting conversation with the manager of our beach club that day. As I reported the incident, I could hear a voice in the background making muffled comments to my father,

Then, "Is that your son you're talking to?" I heard Dad reply, "Yes," and continued,

"I may have to get a lawyer to get my money back."

"Where is this place? In Connecticut? It doesn't sound like you'll get your money back so quickly."

"No, it's in New Rochelle, but no matter where it is, it's going to cost me legal fees."

"Well, at least it's in Westchester."

The voice in the background interrupted my father,

"New Rochelle. Where in New Rochelle?"

I overheard that and told my father, "The Eldorado Beach Club." He repeated this to the other person in the room. I was trying to make out what the other man was saying when my father abruptly ended our conversation,

"I have to go, Frankie."

After dinner, my wife and I were having coffee on the deck when the phone rang again. To my amazement, it was a completely apologetic Mr. Harold on the other end of the line.

"Mr. Lucido, this is Harold from the Eldorado Beach Club. I'm going to issue a full refund to you. There will be no charge for the first two weeks, and the entire cabana is yours. You and your family will be my guests for the summer. My sincere apology to you and your wife. Please take me up on my invitation. Have a good evening and good night, Mr. Lucido."

My wife and I were stunned at his complete about-face. She's a third-generation Italian-American raised in a middle-class suburban home with absolutely no personal exposure to organized crime. She burst out laughing.

"Mafia wife! Mafia wife!"

We knew immediately my father had something to do with this. I called him at his apartment and asked him flatly,

"Dad, did you have a role in this?"

"Yes, Frankie. When I called you, I was at Little Phil's club in the neighborhood, and he listened to our conversation. As soon as he heard it was the Eldorado Beach Club, he signaled me to cut the call short, and that's why I had to go. Little Phil was pissed off because the Eldorado is one of his clubs. Harold is one of his underlings. In my presence, he called Harold and came down on him in such a way that there was no need to repeat it on the phone. He made it clear that the Lucidos are his personal friends and that he is to give them a full refund and offer them a free pass anytime they want to come to the club.

We took Mr. Harold up on his offer. I forgot about my ulcer and was able to enjoy the rest of the summer. That afternoon, it was hard not to appreciate Charlie Beans' age-old connections. I never did know little Phil's last name.

A Time For Forgiveness

On a Sunday in July 1998, Charlie Beans called me to stop by his apartment. It must have been urgent because old habits never died. Dating back to his youth in East Harlem, important things had to be communicated in person. His large studio apartment was on the ninth floor and had a full view of The Bronx Zoo. When I arrived, he was sitting in a wheelchair, peeling a large orange. Absent from his face was his usual welcoming smile that was part of his gregarious personality.

"Dad, what happened? Why are you in a wheelchair?"

Looking at me wearily, he replied,

"A couple of weeks ago, I tripped and fell while playing pool. I have some fractures. Now I have trouble walking."

He continued peeling. After some talk about his health and my reprimanding him for not telling me earlier of his accident, I noticed he wasn't smoking. The apartment no longer had its usual stale smell of cigarette smoke. I asked him,

"Dad, after all these years, why did you stop smoking?"

"Frankie, when the pain of the cough was greater than the pleasure of the cigarette, I stopped smoking. Everything has changed. It's killing me. I don't go out anymore because I don't want people seeing me wheeling along 187th Street to get to the club or even to the grocery store. I can't even go to the pool room to hang out with the guys anymore. There's no elevator in Pop's or Tally's poolroom. I'm ready to pack it in."

This was not the ever-resilient Charlie Beans I knew.

"Dad, you're depressed. Give it some time. You'll work it out. You're not a quitter! When do you see the doctor again?"

"He's coming here on Thursday morning."

"Okay. I'll come by early with coffee and pastries from Artuso's."

"Frankie, listen to me. Go into the closet. There's a plaid jacket there. In the breast pocket, there is some money. Bring it to me."

His large walk-in closet held many suits and jackets neatly hung on one side, with shirts, slacks, and sweaters on the other side. Slipping my hand between the crowded pieces of clothing, I located the almost hidden plaid jacket. I pulled out the five crisp new $20 bills I found there, as instructed, and gave them to him. Carefully fanning them like poker cards in his hand, he took the first bill and placed it in my hand.

"This Is for Paul."

Separating the second bill, he handed it to me,

"This is for David."

He gave me the remaining three twenties. Our eyes met. With eyes glistening, he said,

"I gave the boys. These are left for you."

Charlie Beans did a lot of careless things in his life that thoughtlessly affected his family in negative ways. This emotional gesture, for him, was an apology. And for me, a sign, it was time for forgiveness. Three days later, he passed away.

CHAPTER 30

STARTING OVER

In the early 1990s, times were changing. My customer base, property management firms, was critically dwindling. Many buildings were now being converted into co-ops and condominiums, and fewer landlords were required to make repairs for residential tenants. Learning too late of what was occurring in the realty industry, I had to sell the Inwood Avenue building that housed my business. I missed deadlines for city, state, and federal income taxes and faced paying ever-increasing fines. My building was in a mainly residential neighborhood, and I had no confidence that I'd be able to sell the property for a decent price.

By sheer luck, before I even had a chance to put it on the market, from out of nowhere, I received a generous offer from representatives of an organization that was looking for a commercial building to convert into a drug rehabilitation center.

They had done a comprehensive search of the area and already had in mind what they wanted. The size of the 1349 Inwood Avenue building and the fact that it was only one block away from the Jerome Avenue elevated train fit their specifications perfectly. They were honest, straightforward people and offered me $50,000 outright. (about $167,500 when this book was written). That was more than I thought it was worth or would have asked for myself. Had they dug deeply into their research, they could have learned how strapped I was and gotten the property for a lot less. Gambling, they could do a bit better. I stalled them for twenty-four hours, telling them I had a partner and would have to check with him. The following day, they increased their offer by $10,000.

Fortunately, I made a financial killing with the sale. I thought this would be the end of the line for my business life. Thanks to Roberto, my best and closest employee, I was convinced to reorganize the whole operation. Following his advice, I relocated to Park Avenue and 138th Street and built a new modern shop, adding top-of-the-line cabinet-making machinery. I reinvented myself as a contractor and designer, specializing in custom cabinetry for renovations of private homes and offices. A successful new professional life was born for both of us. Roberto was with me throughout the forty-five years I was in business, and we remain good friends to this day.

PETER PICCIANO

CHAPTER 31

PIERMONT

I've always felt exceptionally prone to coincidence in my life, but an early summer evening outing in 1999 proved to be the ultimate experience. My wife wanted to take the one-hour ride from our home in Westchester County to Piermont, New York, to enjoy this July evening. I felt oddly troubled as we set out. To make her happy, I reluctantly agreed to the trip. Driving south on Route 9-W, the strange mood I was in began to feel more like fear. Reaching the winding road, with its hairpin turns leading down to the picturesque village, an eerie feeling came over me.

It appeared from nowhere, and I entered Piermont in a trance-like state. Visitors go there to enjoy its many antique shops, boating, outdoor dining, and peaceful views of the Hudson River. In marked contrast to my unsettled feelings, I found the streets were lined with lively people having a good time. Children were everywhere. Parents pushed strollers; assorted folks went in and out of shops. Men and women of various ages were standing in lines at restaurants, and kids were playing in the parks.

We finally found a parking space and drifted from restaurant to restaurant, hearing the same refrain:

"No table available for at least an hour."

We decided to try one last restaurant that we had avoided at first because it was right on the river with the best views, and we thought we had little chance of getting a table. Working our way to the reservation desk, I could feel the presence of a man right at my back. The frazzled hostess suddenly appeared from behind a bunch of people waiting for their tables and asked if we were together. I shook my head, "No." She told us there were only two tables left but in the smoking area near the bar. Not smokers, we decided to pass.

Almost bowing, the man behind me reached forward, displaying a pack of Lucky Strikes on his open palm. There was something familiar about the gesture I couldn't quite place.

"If you're not taking the table, would you mind if we do?"

"Not at all!" I replied.

Before the hostess escorted the couple to their table, she suggested we wait until after she seated them. On her return, she took us by surprise by offering to hold the other table for fifteen minutes, just in case we changed our minds. We thanked her and made our way out. Barely a minute later, back on the street, my wife said, "Let's live with the smoking. At least we'll have a seat."

"That was fast!" The smiling hostess welcomed us and took us to our table. It was not just any old table. It was tucked away in a separate, cozy wood-paneled alcove behind an oak archway. The narrow space had room for only two tables, set diagonally apart, creating a zigzag path for the waiter.

The other couple was seated at the rear table, and we were at the front. The man appeared to be around my age. I'd noticed before he had graying hair and blue eyes, just like me. His cutoff jeans and white T-shirt seemed too casual for this particular restaurant, but the woman was dressed more appropriately. She had short blond hair and wore a simple white dress. As I seated myself with my back to him, the man called out to us,

"I think you made the right decision. This is unbelievable! We have this great room all to ourselves."

My wife was quick to reply,

"Wow! This place is well-ventilated. I can hardly smell any cigarette smoke." This started some light conversation between my wife and the couple. My wife is a small talk expert and would make a great talk show host. My uneasy mood and mysterious, restless feeling still lingered, and I was uncharacteristically silent. My wife kept up the conversation,

"What brings you here today?"

"We were planning on going to Battery Park City for dinner but changed our plans."

"Changed your plans? That's a big change in distance."

"Yes, I know. We decided to come here because my boyfriend furnished the tables for this restaurant."

"Where do you live?" asked my wife.

"I live in Manhattan, and my boyfriend lives in The Bronx."

Hearing that the man was from The Bronx, I perked up somewhat, but not enough to lift my mood, even though I usually would never miss an opportunity to reminisce with a fellow Bronxite. My wife persisted,

"Really? Where in Manhattan do you live?"

"I actually live in Battery Park City."

My wife pressed on, nosily,

"May I ask you what you do for a living?"

"Sure, I'm a personal assistant."

"No kidding! Anyone famous?"

"Actually, yes. I work for Armand Assante, the movie actor."

Needless to say, this started more chit-chat between the women. After leaving me in peace for a few minutes, my wife said to me, loud enough for all to hear,

"What's wrong with you? You never pass up a conversation with another Bronxite!" Then, slightly louder, she turned to the man,

"My husband is from The Bronx, and I'm surprised he hasn't grilled you yet." The man laughed, replying,

"People from The Bronx rarely pass up a chance to talk about old times." Finally, to be polite, I spoke,

"Do you manufacture restaurant tables?" "Yes, I do."

"Where is your shop?"

"Oh, in an out-of-the-way location in the South Bronx." Now, I was interested because I had a custom cabinet business at 2445 Park Avenue, just north of 138th Street.

"Where exactly is your place?" I asked.

"I'm on 138th Street."

In Bronx terms, my place of business could be described that way, too,

"You're kidding! My shop is on 138th Street! What's your address?"

"Twenty-four, forty-nine Park Avenue," he answered.

I was floored.

"My God, what a coincidence. We're next-door neighbors. I can't believe it!

Where do you live?" I asked.

"I live in the Country Club Road section of The Bronx."

"Where are *you* from?"

"I live in Ardsley now. But I'm from Arthur Avenue, born and raised there!"

"Go on! That's where I grew up."

My eyes widened, What's your name?"

"My name is Peter Picciano."

"Picciano? Are you related to Eddie Picciano?"

"Yes, I am," he cried out. "Eddie Picciano is my father!"

Getting excited, I responded,

"My father was a close friend of Eddie Picciano."

Suddenly, it came to me. This man's deferential attitude and gesture reminded me of the apologetic, respectful manner residents of Little Italy use when asking for favors from the local wise guys.

Peter stared at me. "What's your name?"

Peter Picciano

"My name is Frank Lucido, but you may have heard of my father. His nickname was Charlie Beans." The room suddenly went silent. Peter Picciano stopped smiling. With one hand on his table and the other on the back of his chair, he slowly lifted himself from his seat.

Startled at his reaction, instinct made me rise to my feet, too, ready for anything. Walking towards me, his eyes filled with tears as he raised his arms and wrapped them around my shoulders, pulling me close to him. His voice trembling with emotion, he whispered,

"I was with your brother when he was killed on Beaumont Avenue."

CHAPTER 32

CARLO'S DEATH

Seeing the shocked look on my face, Peter gently separated himself from me and settled me into my seat. He quickly slid his chair over to my table as his girlfriend moved to sit near my wife. Peter dried his eyes with a wrinkled handkerchief. Now more composed, he launched into this narrative:

"Frank, Carlo was a good friend of mine. I'll never forget that day. By coincidence, we were wearing the same striped short-sleeved shirts. I had to deliver an envelope to a bookie at the top of the Beaumont Avenue hill, near 183rd Street. As I came close to my stop, I ran into Carlo, setting up his homemade scooter. Like many in the neighborhood, his scooter was made from a wooden crate, nailed to a 2x4 with skate wheels attached to both ends. He was getting ready to skate down the 250-foot hill to 187th Street. He called out to me,

"Come on, hang on with me!"

"I hollered back. Hold on, wait for me. I'll be right there!" My errand only took a minute or two. Your brother was a headstrong, somewhat reckless kid. He couldn't wait. When I came out to join him, he had already started the descent to 187th Street. I watched him zooming down the hill. Just before he reached 187th Street, he lost control of his scooter, couldn't stop, and ran head-on under the wheels of a truck backing up. He died instantly. My mother was in my father's luncheonette on 187th Street. She heard the commotion and came out from behind the counter. Seeing an unidentifiable child with a striped shirt under the wheels of a truck, she was horrified and panicked until she saw me running down the street after Carlo. His daredevil ways saved my life. I was definitely going to piggyback with him down the hill!"

Visibly upset, Peter paused to collect himself. I was spellbound, hearing these facts for the first time. Even my wife listened intently. I never talked about my brother's death. By then, it had become clear to me that the peculiar mood I'd been in all evening foretold this extraordinary encounter with Peter Picciano and its revelations about the most painful and significant event of my early childhood.

CHAPTER 33

THE POLE VAULT

I had never been told the details about my brother's tragic death at the age of seven. I was four years old when he died, and I still have vivid memories of the bewildering events of that day.

To prevent our pleasant encounter from becoming unbearably somber, Peter insisted that we order after-dinner drinks. I settled for another espresso with anisette, and my wife agreed to a liqueur of some sort. Peter had a vast amount of Bronx lore and knowledge of neighborhood people and places, and the conversation soon flowed easily. Sipping my coffee, I was dumbstruck when I heard,

"Frank, you know that I was there when your father pole vaulted into Pop's poolroom."

Before he could utter another word, my wife blurted out,

"Cut it out. I've heard enough of these bullshit Charlie Beans stories!" I raised my open palms defensively before admitting,

"I never told you this story because I didn't believe it myself." Peter interrupted, "No, this is absolutely true. I was there with my father and uncles. Charlie was the best athlete in the neighborhood and was always dreaming up schemes to bet on."

Peter was eager to share his recollection of the event, and I could tell my wife's interest was now heightened. It was time for her to hear this famous story.

I stepped into the conversation,

"Pop's poolroom was on the second floor of a two-story building directly across the street from 707 E.187th Street, where my family lived. Peter's father's luncheonette was on the street level. As Peter described it, on Sundays, the guys usually hung out in front of his dad's place before dinner and often into the night."

Peter continued;

"One afternoon, before dinner, word went out that Charlie Beans was betting that he could pole vault into Pop's poolroom. They were always losing crazy bets to him, and now, at last, it was time to put Beans in his place."

Always the skeptic, my wife interrupted,

"Oh really? Where did he get a vaulting pole?"

Peter explained,

"Pop's poolroom, just like all the schoolrooms in the neighborhood, had seven-foot windows that you would open with one of those tall poles with a hook on top. Pop's had several of these poles. There must have been thirty or forty neighborhood guys standing around. Even wives and kids were there to witness the show."

Once again, my wife cut in, but this timeless cynically,

"If there were that many people, what about traffic?"

"Let me finish. Remember, our neighborhood was an enclave unto itself," Peter explained to my wife. "The law had very little input on things that went on there. The cops looked the other way while the wise guys policed the area. The neighborhood didn't have muggings, burglaries, or thefts because bad guys knew better."

Peter continued, "That memorable Sunday," he recounted, "the men formed two parallel lines on 187th Street, closing it off and creating a clear path between Beaumont and Crotona Avenues. All traffic came to a halt, and even the busses had to stop.

Charlie told everyone that in order for him to win the bet, he would only have to land on the sill of the open poolroom window and remain there for one minute. Most of the guys were sure he would end up in the hospital because this was undoubtedly impossible. This time, the odds were finally in their favor, they thought. The street was bustling with gamblers and bookies, and even some of the neighborhood women were placing bets. The cars in front of my father's place were made to leave."

Relishing his story, Peter went on, "An excited crowd had formed around my father's luncheonette when Charlie appeared on the sidewalk in front of his building! Grasping one of the window poles from Pop's poolroom, he tilted it towards him like a pole vaulter and began to run, clearing the curb and quickly accelerating while aiming the tip of the pole at a tree cutout in the sidewalk across the street. In a split second, the tip of the pole was wedged into the dirt, and Charlie quickly climbed it, hand over hand, propelling himself up and onto Pop's window sill. All this, in the blink of an eye! He suffered some minor bruises but told us it was well worth it. Not only did he win a ton of money, he became a neighborhood legend. Even the biggest losers, the bookies, were cheering!" Now beaming, Peter added,

"Frank, I was there! It was like a movie. Along with everyone else, I couldn't believe what I'd just seen with my own eyes. It was an incredible stunt. People still talk about it today! Especially *my* father. Like yours, he made a fortune that day!"

An Offer I Could Refuse

We paid our bills. Standing by the tables, readying our goodbyes, Peter stopped me.

"I'm so happy I met you here tonight. Even though this was our first meeting, I feel as if we've been re-united. Please stay another few minutes. I have something to offer you."

We sat down again, and I said,

"It's obvious that we share some history. You're almost like a missing family member. But I don't understand what you mean by an offer."

"Frank, I am going out of business. Although I have work coming in, I am severely undercapitalized and have no way of making it better. All the contents of my building, machinery, lumber, and hand tools, are worth over 70K. I was planning to walk away from everything until this evening. If you can swing as little as 5K, it's all yours.

And if you can't, it's still yours!"

I looked into his eyes and felt his desperation. I paused to gather my thoughts. "Peter, couldn't you get a loan or find a partner?"

"I've tried everything. My banks won't help. I have approached people to either sell or take in a partner without any luck."

After giving it some thought, I answered,

"I'll tell you what, Peter. I will accept your offer with one condition: Place an advertisement in the New York Times for two weeks for a backer or partner. If it doesn't pan out, I'll have the 5K for you."

"Do you really think this can help?"

"I don't know. But what's the harm? You have nothing to lose at this point."

I got up from my chair and extended my arms for a farewell embrace. We hugged and kissed each other on the cheek. I asked him to keep me posted. We all walked out together, then went our separate ways.

Preoccupied with my own business, I forgot about Peter Picciano. One morning, while turning the key to my office door, from the corner of my eye, I caught the slow closing of a door at Peter's place. I turned my head, curious, wondering whatever had happened to Peter Picciano. I took a few steps to his shop and knocked on his door. Getting no answer, I then took my large car key out of my pocket and repeatedly rapped on the metal door. Finally, the door opened just enough to hear a voice. Mumbling through the crack in the door, a man with a thick

Yiddish accent spoke:
"Vut you vant?"
"Is Peter Picciano here?"
"No Peter here. Who vants to know?"
"I'm your neighbor and a friend of his."
"Peter no here now. He be back later."
"Can you tell him that Frank stopped by?

He pulled the door shut in my face without answering. At 3 pm, I was finishing my day, ready to leave for home, when I was startled by an insistent tapping on my office door. As I turned the knob to unlatch the lock, the door was pulled open.

Standing there was Peter Picciano, so eager to see me he almost collided with me as he rushed into my office, forcing me to step back. Bright-eyed and grinning from ear to ear, he clasped me in both arms, almost raising me off the ground, and kissed me.

Talking fast, almost in one breath, he said,

"Frank, can you forgive me for not getting back to you? You saved my business! You were right! I placed the ad that Monday after we met, and the only call that came in was from this old Jewish guy from Brooklyn. He was a retired businessman for over a year and was going stir-crazy. He saw my ad, and now I have a fucking wonderful partner!"

He sat himself down on the guest chair in my office, hands on his knees, palms down, his head bowed. I saw tear drops falling from his eyes. The small droplets looked like brown stains on his tan shirtsleeve. He slowly raised his head and looked up at me with a warm smile. Shaking his head in disbelief, he laughed softly,

"And to think, I wasn't planning to go to Piermont that day."

I smiled to myself and nodded in agreement. I was convinced it was fate that placed both of us in that small town on the Hudson that summer day.

SICILIAN ROUTES

CHAPTER 34

HERITAGE

In 1970, I was twenty-seven years old. The now classic movie, The Godfather, based on Mario Puzo's best-selling novel, had not yet been released. I had recently seen Frank Sinatra, my favorite singer, perform at a concert to benefit an Italian-American organization, and it sparked an interest in me to learn more about my heritage. Up until a few years before, when a local Mafia boss violently cursed out my father in front of me, I had a mostly positive view of the mob. They were omnipresent where I grew up. Projecting a disarming charm and sense of protective kindness, they made us all feel safe from the world outside of Little Italy. To a great extent, that was the reality. There were few, if any, crimes against neighbors and friends in the area. In fact, there was a general assumption that if any member of The Bronx Little Italy community requested protection of any kind, it would be granted. Most outsiders were unaware that the Mafia also provided small, no-interest loans to local shopkeepers and businesses and others who asked. They were considered family to the guys who ran our part of the world.

I called my father to find out more about my Sicilian background and made a date to visit him at his apartment. When the day came, I was prepared with questions about Charlie Beans' early childhood in the Old Country. But before I could get started, he jumped right into his still-searing memories of being terribly poor and hungry. He told me there were times when all the family had to eat wild greens his mother would pick from the fields around the house. Etched in his mind forever was the evening his father brought home a rabbit and a loaf of bread. His mother cooked up a meal that felt like a feast. At least one cousin was also present to share the bounty. At the end of this festive occasion, his mother had just placed the last tiny bit of rabbit on his plate when suddenly his cousin reached over and thrust his fork into that morsel and tried to grab it for himself. Without thinking, young Biagio lifted his fork and stabbed the top of his cousin's hand with all his strength. His father's reaction was equally swift; he punished his son with a serious beating. My Dad's other vivid memory of his impoverished childhood had to do with his after-school activities with his friends. These young boys would look for dead bodies of Mafia victims in the surrounding countryside, hoping to find items on them they could use or sell. I had barely absorbed these harrowing events before my father delivered an even bigger bombshell:

"Frankie, I never told you this, but the man you knew as Grandpa Frank was not your grandfather. He was your great uncle. His younger brother, Carlo, was my real father, your true grandfather. Your brother was named after him. It was no coincidence that the American name I was given on the boat was "Charles."

Then he stunned me again with this story, as told to him by the man who raised him: Carlo was climbing fast in the Mafia, and although Frank, known as Francesco at the time, was himself a low-level *mafioso* as a young man, he was well aware that his hometown and its environs were dangerous hotbeds of competitive gangsters.

I was mesmerized as Dad continued the tale of his real father. According to family lore, Carlo was summoned to call on his *Don* at his home. This powerful man lived behind a large stone wall and entered through a pair of wooden doors set within a big archway, beyond which stood an imposing villa. There was a balcony inside the wall above the doors. As Carlo passed through the open doors, two assassins were waiting above the balcony. One held a garden hoe; the other, a *lupara,* the Sicilian sawed-off shotgun often used in vendettas. The top of my grandfather's head was sliced open by the garden hoe, and a shot from the *lupara* finished him off. Dad paused to tell me he had no idea what caused the ambush and hit.

Francesco most likely knew it would only be a matter of time before they would come after him, too. With cousins in Brooklyn ready to help him, he wasted no time leaving Sicily for New York City. Around the same time, his widowed sister-in-law, Vitina, along with her seven-year-old son, Biagio, and her sister, Vincenza, also left the country. The women, with the small boy, arrived in New York on December 23, 1919, and went to live with their father, Saverio Costa, who had emigrated to the States in 1904.

Eight months later, on September 12, 1920, Francesco and Vitina were married. They raised my father along with a daughter of their own, who came later, my Aunt Frances.

I remember my Grandpa Frank as a quiet man, a formal figure with a certain air of self-confidence and strength. When visiting us on Sundays, I recall how my mother and father yielded their authority to him. I can picture him to this day. While Mom's meat sauce simmered on the stove, he sat alone at the dinner table in his black suit, vest, and tie. Sipping a glass of red wine, he methodically turned the pages of the Italian-American newspaper, *Il Progresso,* periodically interrupting his reading to get up and taste, then stir, the gravy.

CHAPTER 35

LERCARA FRIDDI

Forty-six years after these revelations by my father, my wife and I visited Sicily in the summer of 2016 with our close Israeli friend, Dan Raz, and his wife, Rita. We had traveled with them a number of times, and Dan always enjoyed organizing our trips. He knew I wanted very much to see where my family came from, but I couldn't remember the name of his hometown. I just knew it was somewhere near or around Palermo. I mentioned this to Dan, who connected with a cultural organization called Mamma Sicily. Although Lucido's name belongs to a large clan in Sicily, I had scant information about my father's side of the family. Mamma Sicily got back to Dan in short order, telling him there were too many Lucidos in the area and that in order to pin down my father's birthplace, it would be helpful to know the name of my maternal grandparents. I gave him my grandmother's maiden name, Costa, and hoped for the best. They discovered it was a place called Lercara Friddi, and it all came back to me. The town was, at one time, a feared stronghold of the Mafia in the Province of Palermo.

The first stop in Sicily was in the town of Palermo. We spent one whole day there, sightseeing. We visited a well-preserved ancient castle and paid a modest fee for a private guided tour that came with an unusual bonus. This *Costello* was once the ancestral home of a local prince, who made himself available at the end of the tour for conversation with the visitors. This distinguished-looking gentleman was surprisingly forthcoming and told us much about himself, including that he no longer had his family fortune and that the government subsidized his off-premises housing to help him support himself.

My favorite part of the day was spending the midday hours at the famous outdoor Ballarò Market, which featured every kind of food one could imagine. As we strolled along its crowded, narrow main street, which stretched for many blocks and spilled into the side streets, we were constantly stopped by shopkeepers offering generous samples of their tasty cheeses, meats, and pastries. Except for the cappuccinos we bought, we did not need to pay for lunch! We did purchase many packages of Sicilian spices as culinary souvenirs to enjoy at home. Hearing the loud, familiar sounds of peddlers shouting and bawling their wares, I could have been back on the Arthur Avenue of my youth!

As we were leaving this extraordinary marketplace, we noticed a man holding a ladle, standing in front of a makeshift counter that had a large rectangular metal container with a lid. Locals would give the man a coin for a sip from what was in the ladle. Speaking Sicilian, our guide stopped one of the customers to ask what was in the ladle. She learned it was a delicacy consisting of a broth made from assorted marinated fish heads. The friendly woman offered to pay for us all to have a taste. We respectfully thanked her and passed on the offer.

Continuing our exploration of Palermo, we went shopping in clothing stores, leather goods shops, and a shoe store, where I purchased a pair of espadrilles. Each time we entered these stores, and later in the trip, our guide, Patrizia, made it a point to introduce me as an American visiting Sicily. Sicilian-born herself, she made her home in England. When hearing my name, without exception, the shopkeepers would greet me with, "Welcome home, Mr. Lucido!"

I asked her, "What's this all about?" She said,

"Get used to it. The Lucido name is so ubiquitous in Sicily you shouldn't be surprised. Sicilians view any foreigner with a Sicilian name as a native son or daughter, returning to the homeland."

On our second day, we got an early start and left for Lercara Friddi. Even though this stop at my father's hometown meant only a slight detour on our itinerary, my wife didn't want to spend over an hour traveling for what would be only a stop of fifteen or twenty minutes. Our guide said we should at least see the courthouse, and we could go on from there. Making matters worse, it took us almost two hours to get out of Palermo. My wife was livid, again asserting this was a waste of valuable time, but she was out-voted. The owner of Mamma Sicily, Giovanni Vallone, was our driver that day. Dan had told him something about my background, and he said he wanted to see the town, too. Coincidently, this day coincided with the twenty-fourth anniversary of the Mafia slaughter of an anti-Mafia judge, his wife, and three security guards. On our drive out of Palermo, we saw a group of students demonstrating against the continued presence of the Mafia in Sicily. Giovanni told us that the killing was particularly significant because it stirred up the region against the Mafia, which had long been in the grip of organized crime families. He was happy things had changed throughout Sicily.

During the drive to Lercara Friddi, Giovanni told me he would like to interview me. I thought it was kind of strange and asked him why. He told me he had a weekly radio program and would like to get my impressions as a Sicilian son returning "home." He had a tape recorder on the front seat next to him and handed me a small microphone to pin to my collar. Flattered, I told him that considering the demonstration we had just seen, I didn't think his listeners would like my story because, indirectly, I am ultimately the product of the Sicilian Mafia. He politely disagreed, insisting,

"Quite the contrary. Sicily needs to hear these stories."

Unexpectedly, my wife encouraged me to tell him about my family history.

Giovanni turned on the recorder and asked me to begin. To get me started, he asked,

"How are you a product of the Sicilian Mafia?" With his occasional prompting questions, my account of the dramatic events of my family history occupied the rest of the ride to Lercara Friddi.

We arrived at the courthouse, where Patrizia was waiting for us. We all walked up the steep steps to enter the vestibule. I was bewildered to see a crowd of people staring down at us at the top of another group of steps. I was about to ask Giovanni if we were in the right place when a well-dressed man ran down the steps and embraced me! Speaking excellent English, he said to me,

"I am your cousin Frank Lo Buono's closest friend, Michael Lanza. I waited for you and must now leave for work. Please tell him you saw me, and enjoy your stay." Startled and confused, as he passed us to leave, I turned to my wife, who was equally startled, and said,

"When Dan asked for my family names, I never gave him Cousin Frank's last name." Just then, there was a shuffling sound among the people above us, and the crowd gave way to a man who stepped forward. He wore a suit draped with the sash of Italy! With sudden applause all around, he opened his arms wide and called down to me,

"Welcome, I am your cousin, Saverio!" He was the Vice Mayor of the town, and the people gathered at the top of the steps were municipal employees, cousins, and townspeople waiting to welcome us! Dan finally came clean and told me that he kept this surprise a secret because he was overwhelmed to learn how excited the family was that I was coming for a visit. Saverio, about my age, was similar in size and shape. He actually resembled me, with his round face, similar smile, and similar eyes, except his eyes were brown, mine blue. We climbed the steps and followed Saverio into the courtroom. The group of family and friends followed and sat in the public gallery. The defendant's and plaintiff's desks were replaced by two chairs, one for me and one for my wife. From the judge's bench, with assistance from Patrizia, serving as interpreter, Cousin Saverio gave a loving, welcoming speech that was so emotional that even my wife couldn't hold back her tears. At the end of the speech, he made a point of welcoming his "new cousins," Dan and Rita Raz. We then had a gathering of my cousins in the judge's chamber, where Saverio opened bottles of Prosecco to toast our arrival—surrounded by Saverio's wife, Anna, sister Fiorella, her daughter Giusy, and other cousins. I was taken aback by how tall they all were. Their height, light complexions, and blue eyes reflected elements of the Norman influence so often to be found in Sicilians' heritage. The Normans were one of the many invading hordes that conquered the island at various times throughout history. Everyone was to meet outside the courthouse after the toast. I remained with Saverio while he removed his sash and gathered gifts he had for Dan and me — illustrated English-language history books about the region. When we stepped out of the courthouse, Dan was waiting to take photos of us. He called out to my cousin to put the sash back on for the picture. Waving his finger in a gesture that signified "no," Saverio pointed to the building and said, in heavily accented but very clear English,

"No. Inside, it's official. Out here, it's family!"

My cousin honored our visit with an unforgettable full day of celebration. Our first stop was a brief visit to Saverio's home, which was not far from the town hall. We walked there, pausing along the way, only to take photos at the address where my father lived as a child. Arriving at Saverio's house, with its imposing marble steps, we were greeted by several Costa relatives who were waiting for us. One bore an uncanny resemblance to my father that struck us all. We then had biscotti and espresso in the parlor, followed by a tour of the small town. One exciting highlight was seeing a

Savierio and me

significant archeological excavation of an ancient Greek site nearby. The surrounding pastures and green rolling hills were breathtaking.

We continued our walking tour, exploring its narrow streets and antiquated buildings. Along the way, Saverio pointed out that Frank Sinatra and I had something in common besides our blue eyes. Both our families originated in Lercara Friddi! This small town had another larger-than-life character. Salvatore Lucania, better known as Charles "Lucky Luciano." Like my father, he had been born in Lercara Friddi. They had even lived on the same street but at different times.

Luciano was probably the most notorious *mafioso* of his time, operating in both Sicily and the United States. He is widely credited as the force most responsible for the creation of the American Mafia and its national crime syndicate. After being deported to Italy, he died of natural causes in Naples in 1962 at the age of sixty-four.

It was close to 1 pm, and Giovani picked us up and took us to Fiorella's home at the edge of town. We drove through an electronic gate and up to her large house, where she had arranged lunch for us and a number of other family members. I learned a lot about the Costa family and their memories of my father's visit some forty-nine years ago. Fiorella's daughter, Giusy, a professional singer, played some videos of her performances. The mood was so festive that after lunch and the videos, beautiful music soon filled the air. Lively songs from Giusy's collection and Dan's iPhone played on the house's state-of-the-art sound system, and we all danced and let ourselves go. It was wonderful! We weren't used to that kind of uninhibited spontaneity back home. Filled with good feelings, I checked with Saverio to see if it was appropriate to invite the family for dinner that evening and if he would be kind enough to make the arrangements. He beamed at me and said he would take care of everything. He made a dinner reservation for 7 pm and told us to make ourselves at home in the meantime.

After a well-earned rest, we followed Fiorella to the restaurant. It was a quaint pub-like place, warm and welcoming, with a bar along one wall. All the tables were arranged on the opposite wall for our group, leaving a small alcove for other patrons. Once seated, Saverio introduced us to the chef, who was dressed, in our honor, in his best chef's whites, complete with his tall chef's toque. We were all sitting, having cocktails, and chatting away when I realized Saverio wasn't at the table. Fiorella told me he was making a memorable trip to Palermo to get the best cannoli cream in Sicily. She explained that cannoli originated in Sicily and that he wanted only the best for the occasion.

    Savierio soon appeared. At a point when everyone was talking and enjoying the meal, Dan nudged me and whispered for me to ask Fiorella, the family historian if the story my father had told me about Grandpa Carlo was true. He was entitled to ask any question he wanted. If not for his heartfelt efforts in arranging this spectacular day, we wouldn't be here enjoying these last few hours with my newfound family. Fiorella discreetly assured us that no one knew what led up to the assassination, but every word was true.

THE LUCK OF THE DRAW

CHAPTER 36

EDDIE'S CHILDREN

Our last night in my father's hometown ended in a late, tearful sendoff with family and friends. As much as I appreciated and embraced my Sicilian relatives and roots, I felt lucky I was raised on Arthur Avenue and not in Lercara Friddi. I had worked hard to overcome the bad influences of my father's heritage and was thankful that there was someone in my life who taught me the difference between right and wrong, largely by his example. I would be remiss if I did not pay tribute to that person.

As a boy, and throughout my life, I referred to him as "Eddie the Carpenter," as if he had no last name but only a title. His full name, Edward Borkowsky, did not exactly roll off this boy's tongue at the age of nine. In my child's mind, he deserved much more than a simple first name. I was bestowing on him a title of respect and a higher rank than the other men I knew. If his title was "Eddie the Carpenter," then his domain was a storefront under an elevated train in the South Bronx. The shop, as he called this place, was a narrow street-level store, lit only by two or three light bulbs dangling from the ends of wires. It was a dark, damp, inhospitable place. His realm was defined by a battered workbench cluttered with leftover hardware parts, dented cans filled with screws and nails of no special size, sash cord, used saw blades, broken tools, and rags. The only subject in his realm was me, a curious schoolboy. I knew from the start that our friendship was anything but impersonal. This was my secret, I thought. From the outset, he was my friend, my teacher, my guide.

Eddie loved children, all children. The first time I learned just how much he loved children was on a snowy December evening in 1961. We had returned to the shop and were putting things in order to close for the weekend. The clacking rumble of the elevated IRT train outside our storefront was muffled by snow settling all around us. An uplifting calm fell over the rundown street. It felt later than it was. It felt like Christmas Eve. As I was putting on my coat to leave, I noticed a small evergreen from the stock of Christmas trees being sold on our street leaning against one of the lumber bins.

Glancing down at Eddie's cluttered desk, I saw several Christmas presents resting on a few letters. The letters were written on ruled paper, with large irregular printing, typical of a child's handwriting.

"How nice. Your nephews wrote you letters." In his gentle voice, he answered,

"No, Frank, these letters are from the post office."

Not getting any more from him, I asked,

"Post office?"

"Yes," he replied. To underscore his next words, he faced me directly, firmly clasping my left shoulder with his muscular hand. The weight and power of his hand were at odds with the gentleness of the man.

"Frank, every year, thousands of letters written by poor children to Santa Claus go unanswered. I'm not poor. If I can make some child happy by answering his letter, why shouldn't I?"

There was no more conversation. After a few moments of wrestling with the zipper of his well-worn coat, he picked up the presents and the letters, turned out the lights, and locked up for the weekend. We were working our separate ways through the mounting snowdrifts when Eddie stopped and turned his head towards me. Without a word spoken, he stared at me briefly, smiled, and waved. He then turned away and disappeared into the snowy night. I later learned that one of the children had asked Santa for a Christmas tree.

As his nieces and nephews grew up, and later his stepchildren and their children, Eddie was there. He was uncle and stepfather to some, but at one time or another, he was father to all. They were all "Eddie's children." To me, he was like one of the classic books he loved. I always knew where to find him and the familiar contents within his plain binding. We were all chapters in this splendid volume that could be picked up anytime and was open to all. The more you read, the more he gave! He was just there! As the years began to pass when meeting with old friends and family, the inevitable question would come up, "How's Eddie the Carpenter?" If anyone was present who didn't know me well, they might ask, "*Who's* Eddie the Carpenter?" Someone would usually answer for me, "Eddie the Carpenter is Frank's longtime friend. He taught him the trade." That's all that needed to be said. I never gave the familiar question much attention until after my final visit with him, three weeks before his death.

By 1999, we were seeing each other quite regularly. Eddie would visit me at my home on an average of once every other month. He was physically slowing down and had lost the usual bounce in his step. Left alone in my kitchen, we would talk. The routine was always the same. I would make a pot of coffee while we conversed. Always the same topics, in the same order — current events, then shoptalk about the old days.

Usually, by the time we had a second cup of coffee, we had exhausted these subjects. At this point, it was an unwritten rule that I would turn the table talk over to Eddie. Actually, now that I think of it, Eddie always did most of the talking. Time after time, I would listen to the same well-seasoned stories about his family, a family he deeply loved — his wife, his sisters, his nephews, and cherished grandchildren. The same stories, visit after visit, year after year. These stories, repetitious as they were, were something very special to me. They were a chronology of my life with Eddie. They were bookmarks in the pages of our history together.

Our last visit was different from all the others. He was depressed. For the first time in all the years I'd known him, he went off routine. He talked briefly about his family and then spoke about himself,

"In this, my seventy-fourth year, I became an old man to myself," he lamented. He told me he'd stopped taking his daily walk and felt as if his legs could no longer support the weight of his body. His hearing, impaired years ago from working for most of his life in a shop under the El, was worsening. Some of his teeth had fallen out. He regretted that he had never taken enough time to write about his life as a carpenter and about the few close people he remembered and loved. He proceeded to tell me the story of a movie star of his generation, George Sanders. On an evening out with friends, the English actor told them he'd had a good life and had lived long enough. He then went home and committed suicide. Eddie assured me he had no intention of taking his own life. He was taking medication for depression and had an appointment to see a therapist. We talked a bit more, and then I ended the conversation with some words of encouragement. I told him that he was a lucky man. Considering his age, he may have been weakened physically, but his mind was as lucid as ever, and I volunteered to work with him on telling his stories about "the shop." A few years earlier, I'd been awed to discover he had actually taken a writing course and had written a beautiful piece about his wife.

As he slowly lifted himself out of his chair to leave, he looked at me with tearful eyes, raised a once-powerful arm, and rested a tired hand on my shoulder. Holding back tears, his voice trembling slightly, he said,

"Frank, I want you to know that I say things to you that I say to no other." As he dropped his hand and started to leave, it was my turn. I stopped him momentarily and placed a hand on his shoulder, speaking some words that took forty years to say out loud,

"Eddie, do you know that I love you?"

Embarrassed and with his usual wordless way when answering an awkward question, he tilted his neck and shrugged one shoulder before saying,

"I figured that much out."

We moved out of the kitchen and headed toward the front door. I followed him silently. After a few steps, without looking back at me, he said, "Good night, Frank." I moved to open the door and show him out. As he stepped down from my porch, silhouetted in the darkness, he turned to me with a smile and a wave and walked off into the night. As I lowered the hand that waved back and closed the door, the sense of loss hit me hard. I had a flashback to a similar silent parting many years before. This time I knew our long life together was over. We had turned the last page and closed our book. I now believe that when close friends inquired about "Eddie the Carpenter," they may have understood more about my relationship with him than I did. My "secret" was nothing more than my inability to reconcile the conflict of paternal identities within me. I loved this man as a son loves a father. On this night, his final visit, he came to bid me farewell. Farewell to the first of "Eddie's children."

CHAPTER 37

ONE CHROMOSOME

From Arthur Avenue to Ardsley, New York, my Italian-American life now unfolds before me. Having transitioned from the toxic influences and low expectations of my early years, I am now a responsible businessman, father, and family man, living a successful middle-class life in an upscale suburban community. I built a home, paid my taxes, and, along the way, became a tennis player. I've changed in many ways, but I still maintain the visceral impulse to gravitate to former 'bad boys,' like myself. This type of friend is the guy who's made it through rough times growing up, is a risk taker, and a straight shooter who takes nonsense from no one. But most important, he's an honest, loyal friend. It also never hurts if he's a former Bronxite!

I hardly played any sports growing up. I don't even remember playing stickball in the street. The only team sport I played was basketball in junior high school. Most of my teenage playtime was spent in a pool room. In 1987, at age forty-two, I was introduced to tennis by a neighbor and joined a club in Westchester County. A year later, playing well enough to be classified as an average club player, I was asked to fill in on a doubles game and was teamed with a man named Don Van R, who was eight years my senior, and a much better player than I. He was fair and willing to accept questionable calls for the betterment of the game. I understood that I was trying my best, and he was patient and encouraging. I took a liking to him immediately. As the game progressed, one of our opponents was getting a bit testy over the way the game was going, especially his errors. After he slowed the set down twice, protesting a point, Don asked him to be a little more considerate. The player reacted badly,

"I don't need someone like you telling me what to do!"

"Hey! That was uncalled for."

"Screw you!"

That was it. Don had had enough. He threw down his racquet and started toward the other side of the net, shouting,

"Who the fuck do you think you're talking to? I'm going to kick the shit out of you!"

I'm from Arthur Avenue, but I was shocked at Don's ferocity. With help from a player on the next court, I rushed to stop him. Luckily, the troublemaker got the message, quickly backed off, and left. As the incident occurred, I wondered what the hell the player meant by "*someone like you.*" Could he have been making a veiled racist remark referring to Don's wife, the well-liked African-American manager of the club? Familiar with the tone and phrase, I'd heard plenty of that kind of talk in my life. Later, Don and I sat down and formally introduced ourselves.

A tough, smart Jewish guy, he was able to navigate his way safely through the violent gangs running the streets of the South Bronx. He had many stories of a misspent childhood, not unlike my own, and of close-call dangers of more recent years. We became close friends.

I was new to tennis, and I was flattered when he asked me to be on a USTA tennis team he had captained. A couple of players on his team were tennis snobs with an exaggerated view of their talents. I was afraid I wouldn't be accepted, but he told me not to worry. If certain individuals gave him a hard time about me, he would deal with them.

The two protested at a team meeting, I learned, and Don told them that if they had a problem with his decision, they could leave the team. When they threatened to do so and encouraged others to do the same, he told them they were off the team. Then,

"As a matter of fact, get yourselves a new captain. I quit the team."

A couple of other players joined him, and he never spoke to the two men again.

That's how our longtime friendship began. For many years, we saw each other every week, meeting for lunch or dinner. Often, we were joined by Bud H, another club member and former Bronxite. We'd discuss current events, tennis, and any topic that came up. Both of them were big readers, and I enjoyed hearing their opinions about books and articles. And, of course, we'd reminisce about our Bronx boyhoods. Unlike most people, we loved hearing each other's stories over and over again.

One night, Don and I were having drinks at the club bar when he asked me if I still had childhood friends.

"Yes, I do. Up until recently, I got together twice a year with a group of guys I grew up with. We'd meet in a neighborhood restaurant where old-timers hang out at lunch or dinner time or just drop in for a drink."

"I would love to go to your old neighborhood, look around, and then have lunch or dinner in the restaurant where you met your old friends." We set a date then and there.

The following week, I picked him up at his apartment In Hartsdale. Driving south on The Bronx River Parkway with Don brought me back to the emotional day I returned to the neighborhood shortly after my father's death. I needed to close his savings account and sign off on his apartment being vacated. It was one of the most depressing days of my life. During most of our trip to The Bronx, Don might as well not have been in the car because my mind was elsewhere. As I passed each parkway exit, I saw visions of my old life. Mile after mile, exit after exit, I was reliving my past.

As we approached the Fordham off-ramp, I was overcome by a deep sense of loss, recalling the day I walked out of the North East Community Bank with my inheritance of $177.50. Leaving the bank behind me and stepping onto the Arthur Avenue pavement that day, I stopped short, suddenly overwhelmed with the grief of my father's death. And something else. I was profoundly saddened. A world that had been so much a part of me had ended, along with the life of Charlie Beans. The somber mood of that painful memory lifted when I found a parking space in front of the Arthur Avenue market, where I happily worked as a boy. Touring the neighborhood, with its haunts and memories, that day with Don was like watching a film of my past life.

When we entered Antonio's restaurant, I wasn't surprised to see two childhood friends, Vinny A and Lefty S, sitting at the bar having lunch. The manager-bartender was also a childhood friend, Joey A. All three greeted me with a hug and kiss on the cheek. Joey called the waiter, "Take care of my friends."

And Vinny added, "Give Frankie and his friend a drink on me." We seated ourselves at a table near the bar. Curious, Don asked,

"Is this the usual greeting you get from your friends?"

"Always! We consider ourselves brothers from another time. You'll see many such greetings in this place."

We ordered our drinks, and the waiter soon returned, placing them in front of us, "The drinks are on Vinny."

I raised my glass and signaled my old friend, calling out, "*Vinny. Cento Anni!*"

Don followed suit, raising his glass along with me. Halfway through our lunch, a man who looked old enough to be my uncle entered and stood at the bar next to Lefty.

Before Joey was able to ask him what he wanted to drink, I heard Lefty say to him, "Johnny, look who's here. Your old pool partner, Frankie Beans."

Johnny turned and immediately came towards me. This almost unrecognizable old friend was what was left of Johnny D, one of my closest childhood buddies. I hadn't seen him for nearly fifteen years. Johnny had run with the wise guys, so I was sure this was why he looked so battered. I got up, and gave him a hug and a kiss, and invited him to join us. He sat down, and I introduced him to Don. Johnny did not look well at all. This prompted me to ask him how he and his family were. Straight away, he described his condition.

"Frankie, I just had open heart surgery and have to take it easy." Don, to be polite, said,

"I guess you had your problems. Do you have a history of heart disease?" Johnny gave this answer in an accent I knew so well,

"Yeah, I got problems. I was gonna fight dis guy, and my friend said to me, "Watch out, he knows Karate. I told him, I don't give a fuck who he knows, I'll kick the shit out of him."

Don, not knowing how to reply for fear of pissing Johnny off, had a blank look on his face. Johnny grinned,

"It's a joke, Don. But yeah, being serious, I had two stents put in from my balls up to my heart. But dis was jus an annoyance. I was stabbed three times, shot in my leg once, and had a skull fracture!"

On our way home from The Bronx, it was unusually quiet in the car. After maybe fifteen minutes or so, Don asked me to look at him for a second.

"Don, don't you see I'm driving?" "Just look at me for an instant!"

At a safe moment, I turned my head for a quick look. He held up a fist and extended his thumb and forefinger so there was only a tiny space between them.

"Frank, just one little chromosome is the difference between you and your friend, Johnny."

Don's simple gesture and savvy remark encapsulated my life. If I were a religious man, I would believe Someone was watching over me. If I were a gambler, I might say the game was rigged in my favor. But once the cards are on the table, you have to play the hand you are dealt. Some lose, some don't. I've been lucky in the game. I'm walking away a winner.

Epilogue:

You Can Take the Boy Out of The Bronx, but You Can't Take The Bronx Out of the Boy

I've always been partial to warm climates and happily took Caribbean vacations with my family for over twenty-five years. In 2021, I was ready to retire and moved with my wife to a condo in West Palm Beach, Florida. Wouldn't you know? Charlie Beans' reputation preceded me to the Sunshine State!

I needed to replace a water heater in my new home, and it took about thirty seconds to establish that Eric, the building's go-to plumber, was a fellow Bronxite. When I told him I was from Arthur Avenue, he mentioned his wife's father owned a poolroom on Gun Hill Road. That's all I had to hear. My father had been a semi-pro pool player who crossed pool cues many times with the famous hustlers of his day — often winning against guys known as Minnesota Fats, Mambo Bill, and The Masked Marvel. These matches took place in the Gun Hill Road poolroom and others in the area. In exhibition matches, he even took on the game's unbeatable professional champion, Willie Mosconi. Charlie Beans was far and away the best player around, but in those times, he was out-matched. Hearing this and intrigued, Eric called his father-in-law, who assured him he knew of Charlie Beans!

For further evidence of my father's far-flung fame, my friend Don had recently been on holiday in my new home state, where he happened to meet another Bronxite, and they soon began trading stories. When the man told Don he once lost a bet to a local guy who won a race running backward against a guy running forwards, Don was quick to respond,

"Hey, I know that guy! That was Charlie Beans, my friend Frank's father."

I've come a long, long way from my Bronx boyhood, and yet it's a huge part of me. The teenage truant from Arthur Avenue couldn't have pictured the trajectory of my life in his wildest dreams. Once I'd ventured beyond my insular environment and glimpsed the wider world, I knew I wanted something more.

With my business going strong, in 1984, I worked with a builder and was able to design my own home in a scenic area in Ardsley, New York. I lived there contentedly with my family until well after the kids were grown and out of the nest. In 2010, we sold our home and purchased a grand two-bedroom co-op apartment in Ardsley-on-Hudson, New York. The classic, gated Hudson House complex stood on eleven acres, with nine tennis courts. Our sunny seventh-floor apartment had stunning panoramic views of the magnificent Hudson River. The sunsets were glorious. We could see the Tappan Zee Bridge, the Manhattan skyline, and the majestic Palisades. From our apartment, we could also see eagles nesting in the forest near our building. It was thrilling to watch them swoop down to the river in pursuit of fish to bring back to their nests. I was elected to the co-op Board, where my construction background proved beneficial to the property.

Eleven years later, we sold our apartment for a handsome profit. With the proceeds, we purchased a large one-bedroom condominium in Florida, with views of palm trees and the beautiful Intracoastal waterway. At the same time, we bought a one-bedroom co-op in suburban Tarrytown, New York, where we spend several months a year.

Here in Florida, when several of my new neighbors learned of my useful background, I was urged to run for the Board of Directors and was soon elected. Not long after, the Board's vice president moved away, and the president asked me to fill the vacancy. I've been pleased to work with this Board and to be of value to the building and my new community.

Life is good. My sons are doing well in their chosen fields. After starting their respective careers in New York City, they both settled in Florida and have homes near us. I am an avid tennis player and have time to play several times a week.

I have a happy home life and many solid friendships in Florida and New York. In many ways, this memoir could have been subtitled, A Tale of Two Fathers. Charlie Beans lived his life the only way he knew how. He was a charming, complex, optimistic, self-absorbed man. An addicted gambler, he excelled in many things but wasted his many God-given talents and wasn't the best at getting close to his children. Fortunately, I was blessed to have Eddie the Carpenter in my life from a young age. He showed me a completely different way to be a man. Wise and compassionate, he was unable to explore his innate gifts properly. If not for this man's early INFLUENCE, I might not have entertained the idea of a college degree. I learned a lot from both of these men.

My formative years were hardly idyllic, but I could never deny them. I believe they made me the man I am today. Thanks to my gracious relatives in Sicily and to the warm welcome I received from everyone there, I am an honorary "Son of Sicily." However, as I look back over the years of my life, one unchanging fact stands out above all — my unshakable identity as a proud Italian-American.

February 2024

Acknowledgments:

This book would not have been written without the encouragement of Linda C. Exman. A former client with a passion for books and reading and a background in the book publishing world, she had heard some of my Charlie Beans stories and complimented me on my "narrative gift." She became my informal writing coach and chief cheerleader on the project. Guiding me through the process, she offered many excellent suggestions, but insisted the book must be in my voice. I'll always be grateful for the countless hours she generously contributed to this work over the years, and for her enduring friendship. Thanks to her, I can now add the unlikely word "Author" to my résumé.

By chance or by fate, I met Peter Picciano for the first time in 1999, when I was working on the earliest stages of this book. A few years older than he had known my family for a long time, and had been a close friend of my brother, Carlo as a young boy. This stranger, who became a friend, revived my long-buried memories of Carlo's untimely death and gave me firsthand information about this brother I hardly knew. He also entertained me with happier stories, including having personally witnessed one of Charlie Beans' most famous stunts.

To validate certain childhood recollections, I relied on Nicky "Red" Aragonesi, my boyhood friend and current go-to historian of the old neighborhood. Nicky's invaluable knowledge verified every memory I had questioned.

In the 1980s, when I took up tennis, I was lucky to meet Don Van Raalte, a tough Jewish guy from the South Bronx who became my closest friend. Through Don, I made many new friends, and these tennis buddies became a willing audience for my stories.

I'll always be thankful to my dear friend, the late Stan Gelber. A well-known music composer and entertainment lawyer, he had seen the initial portions of my manuscript and never stopped applauding my efforts. It was Stan who used "A Tale of Two Fathers" to describe my life story.

Special thanks must be reserved for Jeanne, my wife of forty years, for putting up with my years-long obsession with developing this memoir. Without her giving me plenty of space to avoid distractions, I would not have been able to delve into hidden corners of my life, and figure out how to come to terms with them. I appreciate the way she deferred to the time-consuming nature of my efforts more than I can ever say.